The Heart in Exile

gift
DrMds

The Heart in Exile

South African Poetry
in English,
1990-1995

EDITED BY

LEON DE KOCK & IAN TROMP

PENGUIN BOOKS

PENGUIN BOOKS

Published by the Penguin Group
27 Wrights Lane, London W8 5TZ, England
Viking Penguin, a division of Penguin Books US Inc, 375 Hudson Street,
New York, New York 10014, USA
Penguin Books Australia Ltd, Ringwood, Victoria, Australia
Penguin Books Canada Ltd, 10 Alcorn Avenue, Toronto, Ontario, Canada M4V 3B2
Penguin Books (NZ) Ltd, 182-190 Wairau Road, Auckland 10, New Zealand
Penguin Books, Amethyst Street, Theta Ext 1, Johannesburg, South Africa
Penguin Books Ltd, Registered Offices: Harmondsworth, Middlesex, England

First published by Penguin Books 1996

Selection and Preface copyright © Leon de Kock & Ian Tromp 1996
The Acknowledgements on pages 330 to 332 constitute an extension of this copyright page.

ISBN 0 140 58760 8

Typeset by Iskova Image Setting in 13 on 15 point Palatino
Cover painting by Keith Dietrich, 'Of Fevers and Other African Sicknesses' (1993).
Egg tempera on canvas, 120 cm × 120 cm
Cover design by Keith Dietrich and Hadaway Illustration & Design
Printed and bound by CTP Book Printers (Pty) Ltd, Caxton Street, Parow 7500, Cape Town

CONTENTS

xii

INTRODUCTION

The Heart in Exile was born in transit, during a murderous daily shuttle between Johannesburg and Pretoria. The editors were then both employed by the University of South Africa in Pretoria but preferred to live in Johannesburg, along with other academics who shared their cars and their passage to work. The daily drive, in fierce morning traffic on the fastest, busiest motorway in Africa, was often a surprisingly unique experience. In the midst of thunderous speed, we quelled our subliminal fears of mangled death by telling stories, recirculating the narratives of our separate lives, and trying to laugh as much as possible. It was a kind of ritual passage, a free space for whimsy and nonsense, between highway's dangers and a morning of hard-to-stomach distance teaching at Unisa. Frequently, the trip was interrupted by a detour into one of the ultra-convenience highway stops which repeat themselves on opposite sides of the six-barrel road. Here we bought polystyrene cups of steaming, machine-dispensed cappuccino and unexpectedly fine croissants. After the caffeine took hold, our conversations and stories became lively, hopeful and iconoclastic.

We had often spoken of poets and poetry, and had occasionally, in the inevitable conversational lulls punctuating the steaming midsummer afternoon return journey, retreated into books of poems or new issues of the few poetry journals produced in South Africa. One morning, as the caffeine took hold, our conversation turned to writers and writing. Why was the country at large, the intelligentsia, even tertiary teachers, so apparently impervious to South African poetry? Individual poetry collections seldom broke even, let alone made any kind of impression on anyone's sense of South Africanness. It seemed only poets themselves bothered, although even they avoided buying the books. As far as a South African culture in the larger sense was concerned, we wondered why 'local' poetry failed to find a more receptive audience. Was it not our particular expression of a here-and-now written in a more diverting and revealing manner than the interest-driven manipulations of advertising, the banalities of reportage, the clichés of talk-radio? Were people really so abject in their submission to the instantly available forms of media culture, or was poetry itself extremely bereft of marketing skills? We wondered whether a more decisive intervention wouldn't begin to make a difference. Someone ventured the opinion that when he arrived in a new country, he needed two items of reading to give him a sense of the place: a local newspaper and a collection of local poetry. Someone else then told the story of a young American entrepreneur who took it upon himself to ensure that in every motel room in the United States, visitors would find, alongside the Gideon Bible, a collection of poems. Imagine that! In every South African hotel, visitors to the new South Africa (local and foreign) would find a beautiful book, a selection of the best poems published since Nelson Mandela's release at the beginning of 1990. The so-called new South Africa could be found there, in a thousand different nuances, in the personal accommodations of an intractable land, in the satirical inflections of such struggles, in the political substratum of daily life, and the many other turns of feeling in contemporary South African poetry in English. By the time we reached Pretoria, the decision to go ahead had been made. We would make the book, approach a big publisher, and then offer it to the country at large.

When the caffeine wore off, we realised it might not be so easy, or even possible, to sell the poetry of a new South Africa to such a big audience. Nevertheless, the matter of audience remained a dominant factor in our conception of the book. The poems would have to speak to ordinary people. And not just speak. We wanted poems of potentially breathtaking impact, poems with sinuous, sensuous textures of feeling and expression. Poems which surprise you with a revelation of the capacity of words — mere words on a page — to offer those momentary intuitions of life elsewhere, other, and yet familiar. We felt unashamed about seeking out poems of enchanting, or devastating, effect. A number of themes suggested themselves, deriving from our observation of poets accommodating themselves to — making certain settlements with — a difficult social environment and tracking their way through a desire-recoil negotiation of 'South Africa' as a paradoxical sense of place/home/land/landscape, from within or outside the country. The title of a poem by the late Lynne Bryer, 'The Heart is Always in Exile', struck a strong note for us. Within this idea, shortened to 'the heart in exile', we found a resonant confluence of strong individual voices making unusual sense of social environment and personal circumstance in a way which sometimes bridged internal and external exile within a shared context of experience and feeling in the reader.

It has often been noted that if there is any common principle in the varied writings emanating from southern Africa, it is our shared experience of division. Our Babelesque language schisms are the trace of other, overlapping sets of disparities in culture, ethnicity, historical perception, political power, education and expressive-performative traditions. In such a context, we felt, poetry is perhaps one of the most potentially accessible sites from which to speak *through* such divisions, to come to terms with Bryer's observation that 'the heart is always in exile,/already aching/for what it has not lost'. We set out to use Bryer's insight as a leitmotif, with some licence, to encompass what we regarded as the phase-switch in poetry since 1990, or at least in the environment of critical reception that so determines our conceptions of the poetry of the day. Our principle of selection — unusually fine poetry — was a result of the desire to collect stirring poems in a book which would reach many more people than does the average volume of poems by an individual author. Our aesthetic creed, if you will, coalesced neatly with a search for excellence and effect. We felt that the overall result of the debate around Albie Sachs' contested call, in 1990, for the temporary erasure of 'struggle' from art was a freer, more capacious expressive environment, a place where excellence could find its mark more diversely. The dualities of the 1970s and 1980s, the mind-numbing cat-yowls between art and politics, the personal and the political, bourgeois as against revolutionary, and the many downstream effects of this public streetfight, seemed to us to have lost their dire purchase on cultural politics in South Africa. For us, this was not a settlement in any camp's favour, but an evaporation and a virtual re-mapping of South African cultural space. Our overall sense of context, then, was marked by two distinct impulses. First, an appreciation of what we observed as a desire for more, and freer, cultural and creative space, along with the disappearance of familiar orthodoxies and heresies — a greater and more benevolent capacity for acceptance, forgiveness, negotiation. Second, a perception of the need among poets to assert these shifts almost aggressively where they had not yet taken hold themselves.

This is not to say we forgot how mendacious, murderous and immoral our public life has been, especially during the transition years. Nor did we wish to lapse into a lyrical delirium as a respite from politics. It was, rather, an intuition that our experience was both more, and less, than the cramping confines of dualisms such as those described above, and that we needed to re-invigorate our critical perception by embracing the full force of multiplicity and surprise in South Africa's many expressive forms and moods. It was a feeling that the most important consideration in our selection should be the ability to communicate about or, more ambitiously, across divisive conditions of all kinds. The fact that this collection is in English bedevils this sentiment to some extent, but that is our angle of vision as editors. English as a *lingua franca* is a problematic subject, and English as a cultural force has a lot to answer for in South African history, but it has also always been a medium of transgression precisely because of its large ambit and its revolutionary potential. When A.C. Jordan (father of Pallo Jordan, presently a Cabinet minister) translated a late nineteenth-century Xhosa poem by Isaac Wauchope (writing as I.W.W. Citashe), the first few lines read: 'Your cattle are gone, my countrymen!/Go rescue them! Go rescue them!/Leave the breechloader alone/And turn to the pen'. This was English carrying the burden of convergence in a cultural context critically shaped by difference and distance. Its various forms of enunciation, in its southern African context, were often at odds with its imperial undertow. Similarly, in the 1990s Seitlhamo Motsapi's poems are a unique appropriation of English (one might speak of his as one of myriad englishes, as against more orthodox English) to convey crosscurrents of the blues, jazz, rasta and other rhythms, in poetic expression which cuts right through the poverty of a personal-political binary scheme and which emphasises the role of English as a continuing medium of what some in the South African context have come to call transculturation.

And still, contemporary South African poetry remains heterogeneous and other even to the compulsions of home and exile, socio-political divisions and their pathologies, and all other constructions we may put in place here. While many poems do speak to the transition years, many are irretrievably idiosyncratic. They will not yield to anyone's desire for thematic consistency, whether postcolonial or political, transitional, or any other category. We found ourselves enjoying the poems all the more for this reason. In our selections, backed up by database searches for all South African poetry published between January 1990 and July 1995 globally, the only constant factor was a relentless and ruthless search for poems of excellent composition and visceral effect.

An overarching sense of the context in which our choices were made, therefore, did not mean that we expected each or any of the individual poets to carry the burdens of crossing, healing or resolving the fault-lines of a disparate South African history. Indeed, to require such an abstraction would create a newly essentialised conception of poetry and its role. The point was precisely that we should respect difference, that it should be a source of hope, surprise and value. The totality of this collection, then, is framed within a conception of difference in South African lyrical expression. For us, 'the heart in exile' came to signify a surprising unfolding, an alternating series of versions in which 'the heart' conceives of its 'exile' in, from or within the imaginative entity we call South Africa. While we knew that we were engaged in an act of agglomerating various examples under an imposed rubric, we felt that the rubric was aptly Protean for our circumstances. We found exile in its traditional sense in South African letters, but we also found the exile of internal longing, whether for a more gentle country or for a more generous environment of feeling. We found a shared sense of the 'heart' as a ravaged and damaged space of feeling, of the ability to feel, and as the need to recapture an unlimited capacity for feeling beyond apartheid.

The Editors
Johannesburg
July 1995

ACKNOWLEDGEMENTS

We wish to acknowledge the support and assistance of various people in compiling this book. Above all, our thanks to Dawie Malan, who scanned databases, journals and books professionally and enthusiastically. We owe thanks and love to our partners, Margaret and Catherine, who generously tolerated our extended preoccupation with *The Heart in Exile* over many months. We are grateful to the lift-club friends who helped talk us into the idea in the first place, Mike Sarakinsky and Professors Keith Dietrich and Margaret Orr. Further, we are indebted to Gus Ferguson, the *paterfamilias* of South African English poetry publishing, for many small acts of support and assistance. Likewise, our thanks to Robert Berold, for being there when we needed him. Finally, our thanks to the community of poets who responded so warmly to this project.

A NOTE ON THE TEXT

The poets in this book are arranged alphabetically by name, with the exception of the opening two writers, Bongani Sitole and Denis Hirson, whose work we felt aptly inaugurates the theme of the collection as a whole. The selections represent our sense of the very best poems published and written between January 1990 and mid-July 1995.

BONGANI SITOLE

Hail, Dalibunga!

Hail, Dalibunga! It's Bongani Sitole.
Words of truth have been exposed.
A bull, kicking up dust, displacing stones.
Dust rises, ant heaps are broken.
A man, staring at the sky till the stars tumble down.
I say to you, Dalibunga, I say to you, Madiba,
I've done nothing, people of my home.
I remember you as a man I met at Mfulo in '57.
I say that you and Slovo played hide and seek,
Disguising yourselves to conceal your identity,
So you wouldn't be recognized.
You're the light-skinned Paramount of the Thembu,
The son of the Khonjwayo princess,
A king born of the nation's princess,
A bright man of the nation's woman,
Someone who stamped his feet on Umtata Mountain
And the whites took fright,
Someone who drank once from the waters of the sea
Till the water dried up and revealed the stones,
A king who did wonders among various nations,
So the Thembu house was shocked:
Saying, 'What manner of king is this?'
I've done nothing, Thembu, I've done nothing.
One day the Boers set down two bags,

A bag of soil and a bag of cash,
Saying the king should pick the one he liked.
King Sampu's son did a wondrous thing:
Good Lord! He picked the bag of soil, and other chiefs
    took the bag of cash!
I've done nothing, people of my home.
One day I spoke, shocking the Boers with confusion.
They said, 'Who's this hounding us?
What battle's he hounding us to?'
So the whites harassed me,
Made me harassed, just like them,
In my very own land.
Alas, Dalibunga, you're a chief to be nurtured,
Alas, Dalibunga, you're a chief to be guarded,
You surprised me, tall son of Mandela,
You surprised me, lash that whipped certain nations:
In consultations with whites overseas
You terrified whites who never talk to blacks.
I say to you, old man,
I say to you, Madiba of Zondwa,
I've spoken, I'll not speak again,
I say to you be strong, Dalibunga,
Be strong, Madiba, our ancestors watch you,
Our grandmothers promised you'd not die in jail.
Bring change, Madiba, things aren't right.
You were raised, Dalibunga, on Dalindyebo's cows' milk
So you would grow to stand tall
Like the river reeds of this country.
The men of our home shuffled their feet:

Cowards! Your cowardice will be bared!
So says the poet of tradition.
Long live Dalibunga!
Long live this old man!
Long live Sophitshi's Madiba!

Translated by Russell Kaschula

This poem was performed in 1991 in honour of Nelson Mandela when he visited the University of Transkei.

DENIS HIRSON

——◆◆◆◆◆◆——

The Long-Distance South African

1

The passage is an axis of hush and gloom running down the middle of our house. At one end the black bakelite telephone rests on its ledge; at the other stands the built-in cupboard, stacked with epochs of clothing and suitcases, along with mothballs and Cobra floor-polish, toiletries and tins of anti-termite solution, all ready to stink sweetly past the open door.

A mangy old settee leans against one side of the passage, with a seat that humps up where the springs are bust. Against the other side, a tall iron bookcase rises to the ceiling, its books squeezed together tight as a trainload of refugees. Night after night adults pause there with skew heads, deciphering all the titles.

It is 1960, the year my parents buy the house in Johannesburg with its goose-pimpled pale green walls and giant tree whose wood is soft as paper. It is 1961, 1962. Still adults come to the bookcase, stop and hunch and tip-toe perilously on a kitchen chair, necks bent under the moulded ceiling. Sometimes they slump with a prize book on the settee, recovering.

But each year there are fewer of them. Several, I am told, have skipped the country. I think of the country as a thick rope, and various adults gaily skipping. I am forced to revise my ideas some time later when the newspaper publishes a photograph of a motor car, in the boot of which the police brought one of them back from wherever he had skipped to.

Meanwhile, those survivors who come round are all sealed into the sitting room with my father. No one is allowed to open the door onto the passage, where the smooth-eared telephone waits patiently to pick up any stray phrases.

My mother is not in there with them. Quite late one night I see her go treading down the passage in her slender dressing gown, past the sitting room where smoke and strategies pile against the door. She is tired and her features are pale as water, the fire of her glance doused. She has become a stranger in her own house.

It is 1964 and my father is arrested. He neither dies nor is he there. His shadow dents the cushions of every chair. Outside, children dive-bomb swimming pools, dogs barb the air with their din. History stops where the suburbs begin.

It is 1965 or 6. My mother buys a set of cups and saucers and stows them away in the passage cupboard all the years of my father's sentence. They are her porcelain dream of leaving, a constant lesson in tenuousness. Sitting in their dark tissue paper they are forerunners, waiting for the other objects in the house to join them on a long-delayed journey to somewhere else.

2
The garden gate is on its last legs. The worn latch hardly holds; one wooden upright, wobbly with termites, is lashed to the same fence which it should be saving from collapse. The ground under the gate has been removed by stormwater summer after summer till any fat cat could worm its way through.

But right now there is nothing and no one at the gate. From the sitting room window the only creature I can see is a butcher bird, high above the hedge on a telephone wire, ticking away the seconds with its tail. It is November 30th, 1973. I watch the gate and wait.

In the garden, the sun drives against drought-ridden yellow grass, long arched leaves of agapanthi and the lemon tree that never grew. Yet another car slides under the plane leaves outside, gets mottled and doesn't stop. The more I wait, the less he is there. Shadows on the meat-red porch deepen against the glare.

I turn from the window to the quiet inside. The whole house has been dusted and waxed till it shines like a bride. My mother has weighed the kitchen table down with delicacies for breakfast, fruits and cheeses and jams. It is nearly lunch-time when I hear the car doors slam.

He advances down the garden path, jacket flapping, arms half-lifted from his sides as if the earth were a tightrope, as if it were difficult to cross over, as if after all this time we would still never reach each other's arms. My father, and to one side my mother, pale with anxiety and elation. And behind them the gate, closed against the minions of the state.

My father, full length for the first time in years, tipped sleek and alien into our lives, my father whom I have supplanted, coming to hug me. I am against him, buried in the good leather and olive smell of his skin. I am with him under the nectarine tree, his smile is ripe but mine is aching and green.

He enters by the front door, and the floor tilts under his hesitant, uneven steps; the walls incline, a brass pestle tremors in its mortar. He is in the kitchen meeting Jane, the black woman who has mothered his children all this time. She knows this is goodbye, but goes on glowing steadily. We've been given three days in which to pack up and put to sea.

We sit down to breakfast, and sky pours at the windows, already water presses under the floorboards. My father considers the feast before him, hardly knowing what to choose. There is no glass across his face, no guard to snipe at forbidden words, no bug snooping for them as they fall. We can talk about anything we want, and for once there is nothing to say at all.

Three days. One brother and one sister return from school to find a long-waylaid father. Five pairs of curtains are drawn against prying eyes, and the suburbs disappear forever. Thousands of books lie down for the first time in ages. But my father remains upright. I find him motionless in the passage in the middle of the night, nine years of absence strapped securely as a parachute to his back.

Three days it takes for the waters to carry us away. They tear themselves white from the shores of the Cape; tirelessly they buoy us up on their shoulders. And when their task is done they retire from the far shore, mooring us in one more harbour of estrangement as they have moored generations before.

3

This table did not follow us across the sea. It occupies a corner of my parents' London kitchen, white and round and unremarkable on its one leg and three toes, waiting to accumulate a bit of history. Meanwhile my mother bends at the nearby oven, slides out a date loaf and announces that it is time for tea.

The other members of the family come gradually unstuck from various limpet occupations that have lasted all the way through Sunday. And before long we are gathered in the kitchen, where the plump, rectangular date loaf sits smoking on the table.

Here we are in our new lives, each finding out what it means to be a foreign body. Here are the cups and saucers from before, filled with English tea-bag tea. We sit down and set to, with a pitter of porcelain and steel. The heating pipes burp intermittently.

Hardly four o'clock and the day fades, pot plants suck twilight from the window panes. The sky goes toxic orange above suburban motorways. We finish our tea, the cake, the crumbs; stack plates away and sit back down at the half-dark table.

Someone mentions gooseberries, and soon the old house in Johannesburg comes up. Somewhere in the garden there was an unassuming bush that gave an annual crop of little papery lanterns. Press one open and out popped a tight amber Cape gooseberry, with a whiff of petrol and a taste of sour honey. But as to the bush's exact location, we can't seem to agree.

So my father traces the house in the middle of the table, with a tentative cross for the bush, just behind it, to the right. Someone adds in the giant tree, the rockery, the outside room where Jane, our pillar of strength, lay down at night. Someone else puts up a splitpole fence across one end of the table, and resolutely replants the gooseberry bush against it.

One by one our hands record what we remember of the house and garden, till everything of import is more or less where it should be. And when finally the wayward gooseberry bush has been democratically rooted, we lean back and survey our bonds and our losses.

Darkness fills the kitchen now, our hands rest empty at the table's edge. The house and garden sink without a trace. Between us there is nothing but a flat dim disk, an indecipherable stretch of water in a moonless place.

4

The man comes walking, tall and solemn and slow. One of his hands bends into a fist, an old fist, tight with stamina and ash. He raises it before the crowd, which presses in on him and takes possession of his name.

The man's suit has an executive cut and sheen for the T.V. cameras that scatter his image across millions of screens. But the set of his face is answerable to no one, more resolute as he comes closer, and more remote.

He advances warily, restraining with his pace the entire procession of loyal aides and gunslingers, high priests, kith and kin, praise-singers and hangers-on. It's been twenty seven years of bootsteps and breaking stones. Out of time with all the elation, he is still alone.

There are only a few yards to go now, the ground widens under his feet. It is February 11th, 1990. History waits for him like a big smart car and he gets in. The crowd packs the rear-view mirror and windscreen; the ignition is switched on. The man is back in the land of the living, his myth is in contact with oxygen.

One long ocean away I watch it happen. Wind spreads the chiffon curtains in our flat; the zinc roofs of Paris are lacquered with rain. I switch channels following the man to the car again and again.

Then he is gone and another man comes walking. He is my newly freed father, crossing the garden of absence to meet me. Above us, a single butcher bird on a telephone wire. The sun is hot but I can't feel its fire.

I am against him and the ground under our feet changes to water. We belong to no single place, ours is the history of those who cross over. And at the docks to wave us goodbye there are only a few acquaintances and no doubt a few cops.

Car tyres stick like velcro to the wet streets outside; windows flicker with the foggy light of T.V. One more news programme and Mandela comes walking, behind him the unsealed door of an entire country.

I pick up the phone and call South Africa. Hello, I say, and the echo of my voice returns to me from under the sea. Hello, a friend answers. Are you alright? I squeeze the receiver so hard my hand is white. When a vacuum is broken, air rushes in. I'm at the far end of the world listening to the wind.

LIONEL ABRAHAMS

Flesh

Busy in my skin in my house, I receive
rumours and news. Again and again I hear
about too much death, too much pain,
too much emptiness, the culpabilities,
relentless causes and terrible ends.
Hearsay comes muffled, distorted,
diminished through the walls of my house.
Busy in my safe place, the attention I pay
takes the form of distraction.
Busy in my safe skin, I attend
with half an ear or heart —
because my skin, from my side,
after all is no safe place.
The walls of my house contain
sufficient travail,
the floor lies ready to bruise me,
beat out my breath. Health, safety,
time for work are not vouchsafed.
I must carve them out of each slippery
hard-textured day, must grapple
with the knotted minutes for those luxuries:
my bare subsistence, a glint of meaning.
This is why, for all I have heard,
I remain, you could say, aloof;
in practical terms, you could say,
ignorant of the struggle.

Words for Ruth Miller

'Chthonic': of the underworld —
one of those words I repeatedly learn
and forget. 'Egregious'
is another, grasped often and then
lost into thin colloquial air,
elusive as the Pimpernel.
'Chthonic's meaning rather sinks away
each time into subconscious murk.
What a word! Strong and black,
like 'coffee'; breathless as
'coffin' or passages in pyramids.
It is like 'Gaudeng', a name for Johannesburg
bestowed by men whose word and bodies
plumb the catacombs of shafts and stopes
that are this city's chthonic cradle.
That's how the strongest sense of things
is often underground, the stifled seed,
like some unthought-out phrase in our debate
which betrays the truth we want ignored.
Like Ruth Miller's inner life —
obscured by her quotidian chaos-in-routine
while she breathed her day, then crushed
down by her death, our ignorance,
these twenty years' amnesiac neglect —
chthonic until it comes to diamond light
in dormant rediscovered poems.

Winter Day, Johannesburg

in bushed and bouldered
folds of the stretched veld
lies sharded
history
thin glass sharp
brittle city

high as emptiness the sky
contains no cloud
no wind

air dry as ore
there's somewhere dust's aroma
smoke of grass

onto pale skeletal stalks
and my glad hands
falls this season's
softly angled gold

Celebration

Thalia naked, two next week,
runs up the passage toward
me in my wheelchair,
laughs, turns, runs down,
then up and down again, again,
greeting approach each time
with glee. The joke holds even
when someone big brushes through
and Thalia, staggering against the air,
raises hands to ward off wall or fall.
I feel safe for a thousand years.

TATAMKHULU AFRIKA

Tamed

You come out onto the dais,
distant as a god, a totem, raise
your arms and we roar
with an adoration like a rage.
But the trees are dumb,
the wind stalled, the air
ambivalent as a new wine.
There should be doves
to racket up in a salute,
but even the pigeons,
crouched on the windowledges, ring
us with their stricken rigid wings.
I strive
to tiptoe, to see
you the better, but my blood,
like the wind, has stalled
and I am mired in the flesh
turned slush of my feet as my fists
pump the air and I shout
old slogans old gods
hear as but the cold
seas' mechanical praise.
Beside me, a black
man in glasses, moustache's

white-as-a-milk-
slick waiting to be tongued,
face falling in,
turns to me his back
in its suit of a fine cloth,
frets behind the glasses, hooks
out a single shining tear.
Hemming me, two
louts with wet lips, eyes hot
as coals a wind blows
to this side of flame,
still their roistering, stand
imploded and intent,
agelessly beyond their age.
One looks up, around
him, seeing only you,
and his face lights
with something of the sublimity
he must believe you bring,
beneficently will lend.
Your hand cuts,
and it silences us
as though it severed tongues,
and I am looking back to the once
the hand held mine
and it was still the man's
the sourness of the cells
gloved with the sourness of a death,
and your eyes were still those
of one running from the long hell.
And now?

Are you still he that,
stripped to his soul,
denied it its death,
sought the dream in even stone and iron?
A mannikin hands
you the typed sheets of your speech.
You shuffle them, tap
the microphone, gently clear
an old phlegm from your throat —
and are oracle,
measured thunder of your voice
doomsday's in a square.
But then comes
the small fumble of the tongue,
the stretching thin
of the fabric of the spell,
and the words are sad
old slogans that fall
like stones onto a stone,
and I see now the white,
imperial quiff is blued,
though the eyes
still scuttle in an old skull,
and the mannikin is feeding
you with more words,
stolidly as into a machine,
and a dignitary lifts
a cuff to check a watch,
to covertly signal now
is the time to ring
down the curtain, move

on to a new square in an old game.
You heed.
We rise in rapture, stretch
up our hands to the kitsch,
alienating pedestal we've piled
for your pinioning, and you reach
out to bless
us and I am hanging my head —
amongst these many thousand others
hanging my head lest
you see me weep,
knowing, as I know,
that there is no crying like
the lamentation of old men.

Trespasser

I wheel my bike under
the cathedral's dark overhang.
Seized by a rictus of the wind,
the trees shed rain.
Rain slides down
Wale Street's sleek, steep fall:
air is an ocean booming round
high, bare walls.
My hands freeze on
the bike's crossbar,
seek the sodden saddle, toy
with the ice-cold bell:
I am suddenly fugitive,
homeless and cornered in
a caprice of pressure and cloud.

Then they cough and I know
I am not alone:
far back, against the great, nailed doors,
they huddle: the troglodytes
of night's alcoves,
daytime's shopping-malls,
parking lots, sparse green lawns,
municipal benches where
lunchtime's city workers, stripping down
their food-packs, sit
in sober rows.

I fear to turn around,
stiffen in expectation
of the inevitable tugging at my sleeve,
wonder if I have any coins,
wonder why they do not bicker,
as they always do,
cursing their mothers' wombs
in tired robots' tones,
why only this
curious, chuckling, liquid sound
drawing me around.

She has the usual wrappings on
stick-thin, brittle shins,
patchy-purple, quietly rotting
methylated spirits skin:
doekie of incongruous elegance crowns
the scabrous, half-bald skull.
Her man, grotesque
as a gargoyle roused from stone,
cradles an infant on his lap,
feeds it from a bottle with a teat,
makes the chuckling, crooning sounds
that turned me round,
that hold me now spellbound.
'Good morning, sir,' he says,
and his voice is grave
as a paterfamilias in his lounge.

Only the odd man out,
leaning against the harsh, grey walls,
looks at me with carefully indifferent eyes,
finding me alien on his home ground,
wishing the clouds would break and I be gone,
ringing my bike's absurd, small bell.

Sheddings

There is sadness in the room.
It lies like dust on wall, and floor, and glass,
echoes in the buzzing of a fly that, caught
by one leg on a coil of sticky paper, fights
with tired plaintiveness to be loosed.
A starling, crying in the empty yard,
turns a shallow silence to profundity.
The dripping of a faulty tap
into a soap-and-grime-encrusted bath
is the final, springless clock that marks
the passing of unlived-in time.

I walk around the room and touch
a pillow, smelling still of old hair-oil,
a bathrobe with a crooked hem, a shoe,
with scuffed, sharp heel and soiled instep,
a billowing scarf of flowering, purple gauze,
hanging from a bedpost and heavy with
the scent of lacquers and stale shampoo,
and, with a sense of guilt almost,
a yellow stain on a thrown-back sheet,
a packet of condoms and one of pills
beside an emptied waterglass,
stale ash, stale butts with old lip-stains,
toothbrush still laid across the tube as though
just used, and I no right to gaze or touch.

And still the starling calls and calls
across the empty wind-lashed yard,
drawing me to the window where
I stand and stare at blowing leaves,
the long-neglected flower-beds,
the slogan-spattered, high yard-walls,
but seeing none of these, waiting for
some sound to turn me round to find
you were behind me all the time,
were never gone, I knew you then
as I know you now,
with a terrible and aching fullness from
these dumb, betraying things.

Shacklemates

You looked around
when they took your arm,
led you
with such a mannerly, mild
tolerance down
the steps to the raw,
slow busyness of the cells.
It would have been better had they dragged you there,
screaming, leaving bloody trails
on the blank, scrubbed courtroom floor.
There would have been less silken menace then
in the manner of their taking you,
less pathos
in your mute, disturbing stare.
As so many times before,
your eyes implored
the help of my then stopped hands,
my powerlessness levelling us
in a communion of chains.
Had you but raged,
I would not have known this guilt,
the long, sad shadow of you propped
against every darkening door, cast
across every steepening hill;
but your eyes held only hurt
of some slapped child,
around you bulked
so great a darkness it was as though

the sun had set,
and the blind, white rictus of your panic splayed
in a gibbering, mad shape
on the noon turned night, shocked
retinae of my eyes.

You will be coming out today;
the ferry will be bringing you in a few hours' time.
I remember the evening we held
the candle parade;
I took the small, flapping flame
down to the sea's edge,
streamed it on the cold seawind,
whispered your name,
but only the sea whispered back:
unintelligible shell sounds.
Next door, the others bustle, exclaim,
ask me when I, too, am going down:
were we not, then, friends?
I am afraid.
After all these years,
will you be the same,
boy or man,
neurotic, bitter or serene?
Will there be anything left for us to talk about,
anything save
the ashes of spent time,
explanations coming now too late,
silences louder than screams?
Will I, too, be freed?

The Night Cart Man

Small town's streets,
empty as beggars' palms,
would supplicate
gold of the moon,
silver of the stars,
and I,
quaking and straight
with terror in my sheets,
would wait for the first
clip-clop, clip-clop,
of the night
cart's horses' hooves.
Midnight to first light
was their shift.
We all knew men
more devils than men
flicked the horses' rumps
with braided human hairs,
clanged up the iron gates
in the streetside shithouse walls,
bundled out the buckets, black
as the horses and the hands,
tipped the slithery
faeces into the tank,
banged the buckets'
echoing emptiness back —
and clip-clop, clip-clop,
the fearsome steps would fade

away into the dark where day seemed
a tale God told
to little kids and fools.

'You be good now,'
foster-aunt would warn,
'and sleep, or else
the night cart man
will steal away your eyes.'
But, one night,
a demon, deep
in my head, said:
'Up, boy, up!'
and I went to the window and saw
the great horses coming out of the night,
black and shining as the sea,
and the night cart men,
old sacks over their heads,
pacing alongside,
silent and slow as priests that bear
their dead to their graves.
And one of them saw
me watching, nose
glued to the glass,
eyes huge as only children's are,
and he flashed his teeth like a string of stars,
and dropped a lid in a wink as loud
as a banged-down shithouse gate and roared
some boisterous as the wind,
taking me to his heart,
amiable thing.

And I stood and howled till I woke the house,
wanting not
this swart as a coon,
grinning buffoon,
but my old dead
scaring the shit out of me
devil-man.

Recluse

I must, they tell me,
go out more,
meet friends,
take in a show;
I am not, they say
a star or stone,
designed to be alone.
What, they ask,
if I should go
the way of hermits and holy men,
backing, snarling, into the thickets of my beard,
malodorous as any den
from the flesh still left,
mouldering, on my bones,
the incontinence of my bowels?
And they laugh:
the coy high whinnying laugh
they use for all old men
who would be stones,
that smudges us with the faint
oiliness of their unease.

I stare at them
till they leave,
slithering their last
coil through my door,

shut it firmly then,
make myself a cup of tea
to still
the trembling of my hands,
light a joss stick maybe,
ridding the room
of their smell,
turn up the radio,
high,
that I may no longer hear
the black river of my supposed
craziness run
outside my walls,
along my veins,
and the last
echo of their insistence falls
silent in my shell.

Aiee! the freedom then:
spinning like a dervish round,
and round,
my worn floor's sweet,
sequestered square,
music soft or bone-
cracking loud,
schizophrenic satyr — half
sprung, yelling, from its lair,
all the dead friends back again,
grinning like so many fools
sunning on a wall,

Saturday night's saturnalia now
all my nights',
till morning comes and my yard is filled
with crooning doves'
liquid sounds,
and I am readied for another round
of waiting for the last,
gentle leaving here —
alone, as now.

KEN BARRIS

The People Who Now Live in District Six

The people who now live in District Six
have abraded complexions, roughly planed
by bad weather and methylated spirits.

The women groom each other's hair, crouching,
combing for parasites with crooked fingers:
touching heads as if to say,

we survived last night. In good weather
they sit along the broken duct,
now a trickle of papers and garbage,

drinking sunlight, unwrinkling,
taking a first timeless drag, talking,
sitting like birds.

One might catch your eye as you pass
and greet you, the manners
of a small nation without bitterness:

about a dozen of them. They sit,
when the southeaster blows, in the lee
of the Afrikaanse Christelike Vrouefederasie Tehuis

    an angular ship
    bearing elderly people
    in gravity and kindness
    to their innocent deaths.

An Advertisement for Air

Poems should never describe wind.
It is at once inexplicable, inane,
penetrating, blunt as a cudgel,
invisible, clad in dust. Mobile
air lacks syntax but retains
a subtle fiery logic of its own;
puffed into words it may acquire
a bountiful changing mould of vowels,
bolstered, prodded, studded
with stops — but words, so bitter
and potable, curious and round
are mostly empty shellac surprise.
I prefer wind unstated, unacquainted
with vocal chordage, the natural kind.
At least I know enough not to write
about the stuff. Don't read this aloud:
purse your lips, and blow it
into a friend's ear.

Magnolia in Winter

The magnolia blooms in winter,
on naked branches. What courage.

The magnolia blooms like haiku written in grief,
finding something to celebrate.

This poem is neither haiku nor magnolia
written in grief or described on a naked branch.

It is written in winter, without courage,
with more than enough syllables

and no naked branches. Perhaps
it is a haiku rooted in a morass

that has overeaten and overdrunk
corruption and covered its ribs too much,

perhaps this haiku is a person disguised
as a poem wearing magnolia blooms

like an old raincoat that should
have been pruned at the second stanza,

leaving the ribs bare and the blossoms
on them bursting purple, loosely falling.

At Night

Light-fingered scales of moving mass,
this sifting of the night wind,
bruised by its own insistent implosion,
unexplained, the shuffle and print of voice,
always imperfect.

                    So, the tugging chest
of a gold-eyed plover breaks rules of sleep,
scratching like chalk on damp deep green;
or the sketched mechanism of women and men,
sleeping or twisted to dark business.

Cages of rib and softening muscle,
their braille-caught splendour seduced:
beneath this massed text of skin and salt flesh,
an inward Stonehenge, waiting for midnight
or deeper solstice.

Syllogism
for Jethro

The acorn falling out of dark summer
shatters sleep; its report is translation.
Perhaps before it fell I dreamt the tree,
leaves crisp-edged, singed in brazen fire.
Now I grasp at stranger-leafed terms,
shifting through dry capillaries,
the ligneous, bleached colour of words.
My fingers do not work, they cannot feel,
if I do not wake, I will lose this poem:
the acorn, impossibly, will never have fallen.

ROBERT BEROLD

Boubou
for Julian

I have in my heart a bush of memories
growing against whispering skies
I return sometimes to the planet's dawn
to watch the sun of my childhood rise

Sounds are rich in the forest of return
sourbush smells and hints of fear
Behind me is the ink of the cathedral
and the soft raindrops which slant the air

Boubou is hidden but his song is clean
he'll be here when our violence is gone
Boubou's song has turned to a call
which enters my memory as I walk on

The light of my parent's house is very far away
I don't know if I'll ever see that house again
But I know I'll hold someone in my arms
we'll heal each other of the knife-wound's pain

Is it a call or a calling, how would I know?
only time and attention will tell
All I know as the world turns to iron
is this birdsong and this particular smell

Boubou is hidden but his song is clean
he'll be here when our violence is gone
Boubou's song has turned to a call
which enters my memory as I walk on

Home

starscape
fluorescent yellow flowers
bush smells on the wind

trudging farmworkers
rhebokke porcupines
iron sounds of the night train

san & xhosa spirits of the dead
tears of long-dead farmers' children
unknown hands that terraced these fields

my castle
has turned to ruins
in this house I'm finally poor

sunlight and rain my lovers
sunlit river leading
wherever it's leading me now

JOOP BERSÉE

Wolves

The night is approaching the frozen landscape;
Stars in their pale, agonizing colours,
The raw, wintry, fallen lake,
Pine-trees in their hungry rows.
The slow snowing darkness clicks a switch;
The machinery of wolves is coming alive,
The empty stomachs wretched,
Bitten by the long nights
Of standing over a frozen carcass.
They stretch their anguished voices,
Sing their prayers into the moon,
To their fathers in the holy ground,
Still alive in the flesh of their cubs,
Asking for a new fury.

Mountain

for Sandy

An oath,
World of stone, grass, birds,
The sky,

Into a flag, song of life,
Its gorges an aria,

A soprano's voice rising and falling
Into a lake of sulphur, cutting edge,

Feet of lava, throat of ice,
Rasping a lake of crystals
Into the night's interior.

A sea of lusty waters dives from its heights.
Flowers jerk in the wind; small children
On a giant's lap, nagging.

And the clouds
Write their philosophy on its peak.
Make the mountain smile.

DENNIS BRUTUS

Goreé

Bring back the implements of slavery,
manacles, chains, the collar, the gouge,
bring back the instruments of slavery
hang them in the forests of the mind
let their windchimes vibrate
in the tremors of time,
and whisper the phrases of guilt
remorse and compassion:
Goreé, Goreé, send back the chains
that our hearts may break
and our tears be unfrozen
and that the healing may at last begin.

Goreé: the island off Senegal which was a centre of the slave trade.

Three Haiku

Birdcalls at dawn in
Wynberg arouse and enlarge
the age-shrunken heart

November 1991
Wynberg

Summer heat has doused
the aloes: vanished is spring's
pentacostal flames

December 1991
Durban

Soundlessly, lilac
flowers drop on the terrace:
butterflies at rest

LYNNE BRYER

In the Archives

The photograph's entitled:
Panoramic view of Hanover.
Some panorama! This is a dorp in the Karoo.

But don't you love the straight bare streets,
the winter poplars like vertical smoke
on a windless dawn?

It's still. Perhaps a cockcrow.
No rumbling cartwheels, not even
a bicycle rushing by like wings.

White houses stand with roofs of tin:
wet silver. Behind each
stretch the erfs: neat
drystone walls, fruit trees,
crisp furrows, paths, the water sloot.

Doesn't your heart leap
for the simple definition,
the ordained, the peaceful
pious certainty?

The Heart is Always in Exile

The heart is always in exile,
already aching
for what it has not lost.

Some words
seem to be clay,
perhaps stone:

something local and specific,
springing from the earth as
— who should say? —
ears of wheat, loaves of bread

tasting of the soil there,
as wine from one small valley
needs to be named anew.

Take them on the tongue: round
or sharp, they're hewn of here,
shaped by a topography
nowhere else true.

Run your fingers over them,
feel the braille
of donga, koppie, kloof,
the homesick lurch
of windmill   stoep   Karoo.

Your heart is already in exile,
it aches, anticipating loss.

Moments at the Gate

Late afternoon, and the pepper tree shivers
disconsolate in the wind. Watching it,
I shiver too, remembering what?
Upcountry farms,
night journeys over chalkwhite roads, the earth
turned lonely as a planet — yes, there,
those moments at the gate — a child,
you left the trim shape of the family car
that travelled snug and lit
as one of those first spaceships, you
stepped out into the cold,
nothing now between you
and the ancient chill of stars;
then came the cool links of the chain,
the gate's portentous swing out into dark
while all the countryside solidified to fear
beyond the headlights' beam:
black trees, a sky, the small thin wind,
and you, deserted on a random
yard of road, still stumbling
to secure the clasp and reach
the open portal, bringing in
the scent of coldness on your clothes
and, on your palms,
the gate's metallic, alien lode.

Mother

Like a well loved familiar home
that one has ceased to see
but as a clutter of possessions,
chosen corners
and continuous backdrop,
carapace to one's flesh
and inward pearl,

You, mother, are a feeling
so familiar I barely recognise
its flavour; asked to tell
that taste, I'd hesitate, test
fabric that's composed of you
and memory, years when you were
ground and matrix, skirts for clinging,
breast (in spotted silk) for leaning
on the long road home on Sundays,
driving in the dark, when you
were not a person but this pure
necessity.
       I found it strange
one day to see you do a handstand
and land back, not kneeling but
turned all about, your belly
proffered to the air, a slice of midriff
bared. Young, supple, separate.

This still stands clear
when other thousand-things have silted
down. We think we walk alone. But see,
I'm still a child who takes her steps
inside a web:
where you
have always been.

Poem for a Daughter

I have never wanted to hold a woman
as much as I yearn for you,
for the sweet heavy weight I tested,
yearly, as you grew.

Now memory is the scent
I search while you sleep at dawn:
is it peaches, wheat ears, milk?
Some essence of daughter, warm

With the musk of your hair:
from that strong blonde crown
that gives you despair
as it bushes and flares, growing low

From your forehead like a frown.
Wait and see! Your hair will be your glory yet.
And I give you yourself at twenty: tall,
fair, and wearing the garments of then,

But always reminding watchers of wheat,
of the farms they have known, and the folds
of white robes loosely waisted with gold,
sheaves rocked in your arms.

A Time in the Country

No number of years in the city can break
our joy in the country, the way
hours are told by the shadows of trees
and which birds are singing
hardest: cockcrow,
somnolent dove,
hadedas coming to roost.
Time here isn't a watch ticking, ticking,
frantic with imported minutes. It isn't even
the old sundial, which never agrees
with the clock in the hall
chiming through the old house that stands open all day,
and the dogs lie sleeping on the flagstones
and the flies go round in circles in the empty rooms.

Outside, the sun moves: more closely time
than anything else, but not the only measuring
while the *chi chi* of the sprinkler wets
the hot stone path; that's also time,
and the plop of the fruit in the orchard, the flash
and hovering of the dragonfly over the pond.
Flowers know, and insects, coming and going,
opening and closing. Everything knows its season,
ripens when it does, and the sound of the axe
rings through air that is neither time nor space
but purity, a place where sound
becomes form, drop on drop,
knock, knock,
this is now.

Love of Hills

Driving from Grahamstown
in the early morning
through hills that are less geography
than familiar shapes, welling deeply
out of myself like members of my own
family, figures not truly separate since relation
gives them unconditional shelter in the self —
I see a field of earth lying lilac in the light,
and on its curve a man with a tractor,
ploughing,
so that a small, far spurt of purple dust
hangs as a cloud.
Then such a rush of love and longing
fills me — joy, shards of regret,
an ancient, fierce belonging — that my breast
begins to burst, unable to contain
the pure reflection rising:
hill, field, cloud of dust,
the whole blest, well beloved
country of the heart.

Release, February 1990

He emerged, walked free
looking like an ordinary, sweet grandfather
from the Eastern Cape:
those lovely old men we children knew
were wise and saintly,
walking down the streets
in ancient suits, greatcoats
from the First World War. We always greeted,
an exchange both courteous and right.

Grown older, we salute Mandela.
Not the bogeyman whose face
was a forbidden sight (abroad,
we looked in libraries); nor charismatic
warrior, giving tongue in blood and flame.

The heavens did not fall.
But then, for days before, the mountain
(struck by lightning) burned,
the dark alive with crimson snakes
writhing on air, black elevation of the night.

Confirmation came
less from our eyes, watching the images that flew
about the world, than from the way we felt:
elated, cool, not doubting this was true,
the destined time and place.

This is the way messiahs come —
when time can stand no more delay,
and people throng the streets, mill in the square,
climb trees to see.
                    Even the soldiers,
nervous in the mob (since they alone are armed,
and so not free) are part of the convergence,
the dislocated, sudden calm of knowing:
This was the way it had to be.

In the Moment

The moment, like a note of music,
leads both back and forth, and up and down,
and round:
Contains all things.
In this instant
thousands are being killed,
millions born.
Many, mostly women,
are being raped or maimed.
Countless crowds go into exile,
fear in their hearts;
others, somewhere, are returning,
filled with joy and trepidation,
regret for summers they have missed.

On a branch one raindrop
reflects the garden entire.
Each moment holds That that is.
Everything, and nothing.
In its sphere,
all things are done and suffered,
all things contained,
redeemed.

Fugue

We live, they say,
in post-colonial dimness,
twilight not quite
a Götterdämmerung.

No longer loving
England, nostalgic now
for Africa,
astonished to belong.

So, once, the Romans
left behind in Gaul,
Britannica,
the children of minor officials

and robust women of a ruder tongue,
saved, perhaps, to go to Rome,
yet in their hearts required
nothing more

than this worn, tessellated floor,
this view of hills,
the scent of known flowers
borne on familiar air,

the peace to die at home.

CHERRY CLAYTON

Divorce

I
There once was a sunny space we knew:
man, woman and child in kitchen, bedroom, garden —
we took it for the daily round.
Lost, that place becomes holy.
That life that's gone was hallowed ground.

I see it now as a work of art:
the figures haloed by light,
a canvas redeemed from infinity,
a family moving through days of praise
having no faith in our trinity.

It's only now that pain uncovers
what we never knew we were:
parents, children, lovers.
Each grief reveals a deeper grief
as we climb these steps of loss,
pausing at each as the past retreats,
sanctified by being lost.

We hardly seemed to value
what now seems rarer than gold:
the daily gloss of the normal —
irritations, meals, connections —
things that had our hearts in hold.

Suffering is all that we know,
all we've lost for good.
The past is another country
where peace was a blessing we never understood.

II
My son is making a collage:
riffling through old photographs
he selects and discards
with a gambler, or an artist's expertise.
I watch him; he's wise for his age.
He seems to know what he needs.

A fat one-year-old is shrined at the centre
shorter than our second garden's flowers,
and around him whirl the generations:
his long-dead grandpa, four squalid kids
around his florid face
like a sunflower,

his father as a baby, abandoned in a pram
squinting at the sun
his own school class snaps
the set smiles of friends changed and gone
into teen-aged, broken-voiced
growth like a gun.

Sorting them is a kind of fun.
The family makes and breaks its own,
like the tumbling children
caught before they fall.
Family life is a dream
and we know the camera lies.
But like a juggler, juggling all,
these images catch our sympathies.

The finished product covers the board.
It's a work of art —
this shield of Achilles
that fits his heart.

Canadian Spring

Helpless as a fish
I'm caught in your net
in which I thought I would thrash.

Peaceful as a deer
stroked into stillness
I've made your love my door.

Owls hoot in the forest
to announce the Canadian spring.
This will be my first.

Gulls cry over the brown river.
The past is the débris of winter.
May I enter this dream for ever.

Dream of a Small Planet

Last night, between sleep and wake,
in that still time when truth may be seen
after much heartache, I saw my self separate,
poised between two figures, a father
loved and far away, in space and time,
a lover whom I must claim as mine.

I verified one by the other; I knew them both
and knew them to be kind.

Like a planet held by poles apart,
I found my own quiet orbit
but the path was grooved in pain.
I had to trace it over again.

The old roads of childhood, well
travelled, but never understood,
and never free of blame, lay
open to the sun. Flowers and colours blazed.

Dreams have led me here, to this
new country of the mind. Nightly
I travel through marvels and miracles
out of the land of the blind.

Last night I lay in a fragile cradle
of self, hearing my heart beat,
quiet, as befits a small planet,
drawing a breath, hoping for health.

South Africa: Memorial Wall

Written after the signing of the new constitutional accord, and to
praise all those who gave their lives for democracy in South Africa

Is any price too high for peace?
The dead heroes gone to earth
still hold their ground.

Rick Turner, the just man
who passed through the eye
of the needle, shot down.

David Webster, last seen elate
weaving in a dance with his brothers.
He lies in a pool of blood at his gate.

Steve Biko, the rational leader
in chains, tortured in a cold cell.
Blood and pain surround his wounded head.

Helen Joseph, her tall proud spine
as she led that giant chanting swag
of women to Pretoria, arrested by time.

Jeremy Cronin, the people's tongue in jail,
his wife doubly absented by death,
soldered by suffering to the black soul.

Ruth First, foremost in courage,
her life a gift to the future
exploding in her face.

Mandela our mandala
of hope and peace
so long a prince in hiding
let out like a shout.

All the dusty desolate townships of death:
black flesh hacked, tyres afire,
hooded men with guns in trains.

All of the weeping women
waiting for their dead to return
to matchbox houses in Soweto.

No more laughing children carrying water.

All of the heroes
who seeded this harvest
deep under ground.
May they shine like suns on the new day:
Biko   Sisulu   Tambo   Mandela.

Longlive!   Longlive!   Longlive!

Double Track

Returning from our walk in snow to snow
surprised by the warmth of the sun on our back
we cross the low-horizoned bowl of earth and sky
following our own double track.

Stirred by the landscapes of memory
we carry the load of our yearning
for a country other than this
without this sun's different burning.

Stopped by a wind-ruffled curve of white
our eyes perceive the Africa we know:
sand-dunes, bristled by reeds, creased by the sea-wind.
The ache of exile spreads its sadness under snow.

Letter to David Wright: 1920-1994

I threw away the letter with the news of your death.
It seemed a cruel joke in a cruel season.
Hard to think you've gone to earth.
You were my father, brother, friend.
I love you; I will love you till the end.
I knew you in your works and days:
I set down these memories in your praise.

How physical our friendship, bodies colliding
as you learned to read my lips
and I learned to read your lines, attending
to the strenuous, sonorous music of a deaf man
who lived in language, touch and tongue.
Poet of the 'ordinary day', earth, air, bird and sky,
I can't believe you've gone.

Sex between us once like a warm puppy's ripple,
no more, then only love, growing
like the rings of the elms you loved
in an England whose past you made me know
like a tree growing through me.
I saw you once wading into a Transvaal river,
your solid body, human and Roman, accepted by the
    water.

'I found myself at 30,' you told me once,
when you loved a wife, beautiful and kind,
chose a calling, translator and poet,
the deficit of deafness blazing into blessing.
Writer at Oxford in wartime, your first poems
bold and brazen, yet colloquial, saying from the first
what you wanted to say, in lines taut as Homer's.

Once we visited the haunts of your youth,
standing there in friendship, in radiant heat
in a quiet pocket of decayed Orange Grove.
Later, I stopped to squat near a garden wall
and you watched, eyes gleaming with delight
in anticipated memory, the hoard we hold
against the future and the fading of the light.

On our last trip to the lakes, your camera broke,
but I hold it all in my heart: reflecting lake,
narrow green lanes, the warmth of your side.
How solid you sat in that car on the ferry,
how quiet and even that ferry glided over the lake,
as you ferried me over Ullswater.
Ferryman, ferry me over the water.

You were my father, friend, brother.
After this parting, there will be no other.
I thought I was saying good-bye to you
because I now love another man
as if one love could cancel another
as if love were not the one unending stream
shouldering us through suffering and time.

The meaning of our parting now sinks in my mind
like a stone, the last trip you planned
in order to say good-bye, for good.
How you etched your memorable silhouette
on Roman wall, Romantic ruin, mythic battlefield
against the windy summits of the north.
How we stood, so close, in the childhood garden of
    Wordsworth.

You were the hermit spirit of England's north,
visioning its places with a writer's curious, rolling eye.
You led me to the oldest barn in England:
the flanks of the cattle shrugged over muscle
in the holy chiaroscuro of that ancient, rural place.
You were Chaucer's sober modern hand
writing out his lines for all to read and understand.

Hard to believe you've gone to earth.
I threw away the letter with the news of your death.
You were my friend of the heart and hearth,
your writing strong and simple, crafted for truth.
You were my father, friend, brother.
I love you; I will love you till the end.
After this parting, there can be no other.

My only son was seized from my belly one midnight
by a doctor who lifted him from flesh and blood
clear and alive. When he left, he bowed
a courteous salute, and I said, grasping
the greatness of his gift: 'Thank you for my son.'
In that spirit, David, I salute your going —
you who worded your wound, making the whole world
    one.

The edges of my grief are sunk now, at day's end,
absorbed in the writing of this poem.
On our last journey, you wept with sorrow
for your dead wife. We sat side by side.
I did not take your hand. We were separately unhappy
for a while. 'You know your way' you said, in parting,
great translator, good guide, poet of the ordinary, eternal
    day.

The Letter

to Lance

I shall miss your spirit.
Distance like drugs disturbs
the steady rhythms of our dialogue.

You slip away snug as a suitcase,
while I grow thin and limbless as an airstrip.

But my fleeting sadness becomes solidarity,
and I wish you handfuls of happiness on your trip:

May your heart bloom like a flower
and your eyes ripen like fire.

Let life unleashed reveal
infinite epochs of delight.

My soul will be in exile
until your return.

But time passes quickly
on this earth which is our womb.

Afterthought

The words of the girl
become the wounds of the woman

Dreams become desire
and desire is doomed to die.

Experience like an anaesthetic
deadens the illusion of love.

In the tomb of the dead
a woman sweeps her blood

in the room of the dying
a child dreams of a fire
that some day will survive

she strokes this nebulous dream

wood by wood

word by word.

Rain

That day it rained poetry.
At first it started with a few words falling;
there fell love, here sunset,
a lark or two, a patriotic sentiment ...
It fell faster; the Iliad and the Odyssey came down
in a sudden squall of dark archaic drops,
the words of Shakespeare fell, the words of Dante
and Wordsworth, of Rimbaud and Donne;
harder and harder they pelted, soaking into the soil
or forming puddles, here perhaps a little sonnet
trickling off the eaves ...
Spatters of limericks, a dirge on the slate path
in front of the house.

We stayed indoors and watched the words
come out of the sky
bouncing off the oak leaves and forming quatrains
that washed the birdshit from the car-roof.
Small words on the windows
wrote nursery rhymes or ballads
that trickled or ran, reforming themselves
in the wonders of Spenser or Yeats' finest memories.

In the gutter leaves, words and mud roiled
towards the storm-drain
but from the window,
through the gathering and changing verses
we couldn't make out their content.

We knew, however, that somewhere
Mayakovsky and Rilke
were darkening the soil
and cummings would help the seedlings in the yard,
Eliot would grow fine roses;
but we feared that Shakespeare and Goethe
would cause the dams to break
spilling their dangerous flood,
ripping at land and trees in all directions.

Through a break in the cloud
the sun illuminated a canto by Pound
near the foot of the young palm-tree
and sparkled over the Mahabarata as it seeped into the
    lawn.
We sipped hot chocolate and watched a truck go by,
splashing Kipling and some obscure triolets against the
    hedge,
leaving them to run muddily onto the pavement.

It seemed to be slackening
so I opened the door and put my hand out to feel,
caught a verse from the Diamond Sutra
and a Latin couplet in my hand;
wiped them on my trouser-leg and came back in
to the hot chocolate and the rain-watching.

Li Po ran mournfully on the windowpane.
A couple of protest poems shook themselves off the
    carnations
and joined a sonnet grieving for death.
We could see it would soon be over
and in a few days
we would be able to pick huge mushrooms
nurtured by D.H. Lawrence
and the farmers would be glad of the downpour.

So we put on our raincoats and wellingtons
and went out to trudge among the puddles and leaves
damp with words
and we were puzzled as to the meaning of this shower.
But when we came back in for supper
we carefully wiped the poems from our boots.

Lydia Lindeque's Story

(She said that it was all true):

Maybe fifty years ago
in some small town,
in a town-hall made of wood and iron
    the theatre company
    performs a play
    in Afrikaans.

The whole (white) town
have turned out.
    The mayor and the dominee
    deacons and dignitaries
    line the front row.

The melodrama proceeds.
The audience,
restless and loud
behind the pound seats,
    are new to drama
    on the stage.

A shot is fired
or poison downed:
an actress pitches over
    sideways
       into
the hero's arms.
    He turns quivering
    to the crowd:
           En wat
    moet ek nou maak?

Someone at the back calls out:
Naai haar voor sy koud word!

The act is halted.
    The mayor
    confers with
    the dominee,
addresses the audience
and unforthcoming culprit:
Behave, or no more play,

and the konstabel
is set to stroll
    up and down
    the central aisle
    swaggering his
    truncheon.

The actors crank it up again.
On stage
    a cup of tea is sipped.
    With pinkie cocked
    the hero muses ...
    Wat is darem lekkerder
    as 'n koppie tee?

The konstabel turns
his baton to the crowd:
    As iemand poes sê,
    slat ek hom stukkend.

PATRICK CULLINAN

The First, Far Beat

In the mountains
the first, far beat
of spring thunder:

thick with young,
a lizard on the rock
moves its head

and in the flank
the quick heart pulses.

The Dust in the Wind

The grass black and a turbulence,
a blossoming
that shakes from the plum tree
clockwise,
that drops a hundred yards away.

Spring comes with its mortal odours,
a flicker of red in the hills at night,
and age is a taste, dry on the tongue:
all day
there is dust in the wind.

The Abandoned Farm

Like two unbroken animals
that will not eat or rest,
we struggle with our love. Outside,
upon the stoep the toy windmill
spins and jerks its blades: tinny,
they clack and creak and may not pause
under the south-wester.

Now the wheat is tawny, rustling
at noon and ripe: beyond, mountains
loom out blue: khaki-dark, the river
loops and lingers out of sight.
The milk comes thick from the cow.
Around the eaves the swallows whirr
and chatter late into the night.

And we are animals of love:
restless we play and butt upon
our mattress, taut and naked we
assume the grace of time and know
it now, not then, not later:
this joy that comes beyond the past
and long before the future.

Sir Tom

No longer seen at office or the club, he was 'retired':
flailing around his Randlord house each day he'd
light his high Victorian lamps in every room
to search for mambas, or he'd plead

for 'sweeties' from his own black cook, who shyly wept
to see his master so demeaned. He'd slaver
at his neighbour's fence and shout that there were
    diamonds
in his rockery. With children he was meant to have a

special kind of sympathy. I was his favourite,
so my parents said, and when we went to luncheon
once a month on Sunday, they'd place me on a high stool
next to 'Father'. He'd say the grace, then punch upon

the table, shout 'my sweet boy' and squeeze my puny
    chin
with his gross hand, while all around us aunts
and uncles kept on smiling: awkward, docile, prim, as
    course
would follow course, borne by servants

older than Igoli. They'd dodder on from place to place
with plates of sugared pumpkin, beans or yellow rice. All
    style,

all energy was broken in that room, the curtains drawn
against the post-noon sun. Talk would last a while

then hush down to a silent, sated calm, so all you'd hear
would be the clink of knife and fork against the plate
as close on twenty people waited till it took
the old man's wit to start again, to speak. It was my fate

that one such afternoon he turned to me and asked:
'What would you like, my darling boy?' Without
    thinking,
I said I wanted toast. So toast was brought. It came
on its own dish and in a silver rack. The old man winking

to the table — for all his children and their children
had paused and now were watching — took off the
    covering
napkin, drew out a piece and lavished it in butter,
nimbly slicing off the crusts. Hovering

behind us I heard Jim, the oldest servant there,
just barely whisper 'shame', though why he said this I
did not understand quite then. A square of soft, warm
butter-sodden toast filled the middle of the plate. 'Why,

close your eyes, my boy,' the old man said, 'Open
wide!' I made my lips into an O, smiling to the giver.
Eyes shut, I turned towards grandfather,
trusting. Into my throat he jabbed a long coarse sliver

from the crust. It rasped and burnt my skin. I gagged
in panic and could not scream while still he stabbed and
   bent
it down into my throat. Some uncle (or my father, was it?)
pulled him gently off. Choked with shock, I was quickly
   sent

or carried from the dining room and put upon
a couch in the small parlour. At the table old Sir Tom
stared at his family. Rightly, they had always known
children never should presume or, if they did, learn that
   from

such babies must come men. But strangely, now, the old
   man broke,
gasping into tears. He said he saw white skulls and not
their cosy, smiling faces. Blue-eyed, haggard, he too was
   led
sobbing from the table. Perhaps, at last, he'd understood

how sick he was and old, hearing Doom's blatancy:
the awful nonsense raving, Hell seething in his head.

Again

Again
we lie together:
holding hands
we talk of being children,
knowing we have come to where
our lives begin
and where our lives must end.

Falling into sleep
I cannot move. Cradled
in that ancient mud,
the primal shore, I know
that there is danger.

And I am not alone:
once more
two fish lie in that dream,
alive and out of water, both
just breathing.

The Shell

Simple, I hold it to my ear
and it roars
with complication.

Now, on the table
it is dumb: agog
with the irony of the ocean.

LEON DE KOCK

Nights I Remember

I remember evenings tinkling
the sounds of children
in the streets. We streamed
from pug-faced brown houses
where dull lampshades disclosed
week-weary parents
settling into the dim orbs of Springbok Radio.

(Oh, but on Saturday nights
our brandy & Coke fathers
set forth on Brylcreem boats,
dragged aunts in bobbing beehives
astride and astern on salacious currents
of cha-cha-cha, rumba & samba.)

We children gushed, twinkling,
into the liquid, streetlit nights
down stoeps across kikuyu past
low-wrought gates — the houses
stood primly back, acknowledging
the primacy of street & play.

(We played tok-tokkie and slang,
crouched in alleyways when
kaffirgirl and her boy
took the stocking-rope
slithering in dusky dark
to be a rinkhals or mamba
and screamed.)

Seventh Avenue, Mayfair (white)
we simply found each other there:
across the road, the Taljaards,
next door, the Shams
(where SA champ Johnny's blooded
boxing vest was on show)
around the corner, the Khouries,
the evening doors leaked children
from 6 o'clock baths,
mobs at play.

(In the cold quiet hours, 2am or 3am,
I remember 'Maak Oop, Polisie!'
and the banging at the gate.
I remember, dimly, the torches
flashed in faces dumb with sleep & fear
hands fumbling in loose trousers
in the girl's room.)

But now these streets are ice,
hushed in winter's early dark.
My grown-up steps echo fear
as I clod down Johannes Street,

Troyeville, 30 years on.
I am scared, there's no fun left
in these frighted avenues. Now the kids
are washed in blue TV noise.
Inside, they're inside. Outside
are dogs and killers.

Our fathers, long since weary
of Oude Meester and Coke,
Trini Lopez and Engelbert Humperdinck,
they're in there too, heaving & forgetting.
It seems it's only me, and my son,
awed by night's cold silence as he rides
Dad's fear and Dad's sober back,
who think these streets are worth remembering.

Witwatersrand Daze

for Luke

I'm trying to find words
for this highway blaze,
asphalt daze; it simmers
blue turning to blur
in waves of haze.

I'm driving, driving
to keep you asleep
(speed sucks you into
strapped slumber,
lips heat-swollen
as you tumble inwards)
I'm driving to batten down
those waking dreams.

I need time to think
to breathe this hot highway.
I'm scanning this — what? —
scarred, pocked, minesand land
so that I can write this, for you,
for me, for a language that knows
what you came from.

You will learn soon enough
this is 'high veld'. For 'veld'
read winter yellow-dun-dry,

'kopje' rock, dust-wind, hard
scuffed land occasionally fissured
by a shimmering gob of lake,
and cooing among the willows.

Perhaps in Paul Kruger's day
it was an aesthetic, a harsh
chiaroscuro of flood and drought,
of cool flamingo dawn
and brazen sunset across
open arc of distant horizon. A place
befitting dreams of unfolding freedom.

These intimations, myths of northern lands,
Trans-Vaal, are still faintly legible,
but not on a day like this
not in the blazing daze of highway
where all that shimmers is Nis-san,
To-yo-ta, Mer-ce-des — totemic inscriptions
mastering the dumb ground.

This veld is also marked
by the scars of a century
so that cyanide-grey, misshapen lump
of finest, asphyxiating dust
('mine dump') defines tracts of earth
spiked by imported bluegums —

they look as though they were brought
to suck up the primeval swamps
and leave the ground bone-dry
for hungry, desperate men
to burrow down, and die.

This land is no longer a sign
of the rolling, unfurling
desire for freer places.
It presents instead rusted fence,
irregular plot, factory, building,
vacant lot, value no less.
We're enclosed in squares & grids:
road, house, park, car, job.

The boundaries have been struck
anointed in blood;
'freedom' was made
in the clash of dreams,
visions, readings of the land.
We've been left with these spaces,
underlined & defined:
highway, haze, a strip of hot,
fast, consuming heat, with no place
to go, but back & forth.

INGRID DE KOK

Transfer

All the family dogs are dead.
A borrowed one, its displaced hip
at an angle to its purebred head,
bays at a siren's emergency climb
whining from the motorway.
Seven strangers now have keys
to the padlock on the gate,
where, instead of lights, a mimosa tree
burns its golden blurred bee-fur
to lead you to the door.

'So many leaves, so many trees'
says the gardener who weekly
salvages an ordered edge;
raking round the rusted rotary hoe
left standing where my uncle last
cranked it hard to clear a space
between the trees, peach orchard,
nectarine and plum, to prove
that he at least could move
the future's rankness to another place.

Forty years ago the house was built
to hold private unhappiness intact,
safe against mobile molecular growths
of city, developers and blacks.
Now rhubarb spurs grow wild and sour;
the mulberries, the ducks and bantams gone.
In the fishpond's sage-green soup,
its fraying goldfish decompose the sun,
wax-white lilies float upon the rot.
And leaves in random piles are burning.

Townhouses circle the inheritance.
The fire station and franchised inn
keep neighbourhood watch over its fate.
The municipality leers over the gate,
complains of dispossession and neglect,
dark tenants and the broken fence.
But all the highveld birds are here,
weighing their metronomic blossoms
upon the branches in the winter air.
And the exiles are returning.

Brush Stroke

In the night a dream creases
you against me momentarily,
unfolding origami bird
in suspended rain, on a bending tree.

You brush beside me, the caress
guinea-fowl feathering my back.
Your dreaming leaves a ladder
leaning against a house of thatch.

You turn half in, half out of sleep
to lipread my dark silent mouth.
In our waking's slow ascent
I am the dream's aftertaste, its scent.

Night Space

The woman takes up all the space.
She spreads her legs
across the bed
as if she owns the place.

The man on the edge
of the occupied bed
can't decide if he wants
her sleeping perfume

or the neat-sheeted tomb
of a bed in a room
shuttered, uncluttered,
monadic, immune,

where all's effaced:
the woman's legs,
her careless spread,
her loose-limbed night embrace.

Inner Note

Like a wishbone
or the instep of your foot

this parabolic love curves,
wings stirring

in the neck nerves of a crane
at marsh's edge,

or bends its back into a kite
arching the membrane of blue flight.

You breathe me out
I breathe you in

the smell of your skin
is salt and tide and tin.

The half-open door
tilts cooler light

upon the floor
and outside sounds come in,

an olive thrush
through the hibiscus bush

last evening note
throating me under you.

This much is all we have:
shadows gathering,

fugitive grace,
and the deep body as our penumbral space.

Ground Wave

Just below the cottage door
our moraine stairway of lemon trees,
strelitzia quills and oleander shrub
steps to the sea and deeper terraces.
The warming wind, concertina on the slope,
coaxes open the bulbul's throat,
the figtree's testicular green globes
and camellia's white evening flux.

Behind the house we feel
the mountain's friction against our backs.
Deep fissures are predicted by the almanac,
earth and trees heaving to the shore.
Scorpions come in at night
for cool killings on the flagstone floor.

GAIL DENDY

Tourists

This is a strange land. Nudged up
from the sea, still uncooked, unclothed.
We can be released, here, quite primitive.

They have wild banana-trees and mangoes.
Strange words like *spanspek*, *milo*,
kaya. The land bristles as though it's cold.

We can be released, here. Nudity
is a long, white beach. And the thought
of emptiness. Shadows are dark, but surely

that's illusion. The sky's grotesque
without its clothes. We watch the sea
turn turtle as we soak these burning skins

in sand. Aaaaaaah. A flotsam salted seagull
wheels broken-winged beneath the sun. Foam
flash tumble. Foam, flash. Like a knife.

In late 1992, two female tourists were murdered on a deserted Natal beach.
They had been sunbathing.

Baby Talk

You're dreadfully calm and placid,
it seems nothing will ever move you.

How slowly you've unfolded at first light.
We hoist your new white sails

and solemnly launch your name
in the unloosed space between us.

You wake slowly, like a breath
that has forgotten itself and thinks

of music. On your slender flute
dark stops float between my fingers

and your small island rings like a bell,
tolls for the sea's tight moorings.

Everywhere there are visions
of pale people with shuttered eyes —

you among them are dark,
a piper shifting sand.

Guavas

It could have been paradise
from afar;
frangipanis in unbottled sweetness,
the sky peeling back for lunch
its fresh blue skin,
a network of ants
chain-ganging
nose-to-haunch
unroofed and touching.
And we have guavas
this year
spreading
talkatively yellow
their paramour buskings
feckle-eyed
frisky
and finally pregnant.
We pluck them
back from the brink of desire.

How sour they are.
We bring rivers of sugar
in clear glass jars.

C.J. DRIVER

Somewhere Else

One grows used to it in the end, I guess,
The condition of exile. One talks of one as one
And writes one's love songs to the Emperor
Who sent one packing to a far-off town
In a province of harsh barbarians.
We know all about exiles in China,
Says my scholarly friend in the grey silk:
A poet's home is always somewhere else —
No one ever sees again the cloud-cloth
Draping the mountain, the white waters foam
Among the pine trees, the bright-speared aloes;
These are the images of childhood, not place —
We see ourselves in time.
                                    Shall I never,
Never again see the lowveld? Never.
Shall I never hear the hadedah birds
In the dusk across Grahamstown, nor smell
The pepper-corns in the rectory sand-pit?
One grows used to it in the end, I guess —
And one does one's best not to remember;
One does one's best to think. One learns to smile
At strangers who stare at one in the street,
At the clack-clack-clack of their dialect.
It is the dust which makes my face look grey,

And the north monsoon which reddens my eyes.
The Emperor was, as I said, quite crazy,
And the fire leaping across the tree-tops
Explodes like gunfire in the black townships.

Aubade

A pre-recorded priest awoke me
Who stayed in bed and did not climb the stairs
Of the tower I could not quite see there
Somewhere towards the Cape Town end of Mowbray;
And I remembered other dawns I'd heard
All those years before, in this fated town —
And most of all a friend who woke me up
To come to celebrate his first son's birth —
And we heard the muezzin sing, over Wynberg.
The ghosts of all the slaves who'd built the house
Were gathered round. 'Champagne for sons,' we said,
And 'Freedom in our time.' The old house cheered ...

That son's a scion of the further Left
In London now; his father somewhere else
High-up now, one hears; and I am teaching
Clever boys in Berkhamsted. We've grown up —
And some of us have grown away, and some
Are dead, and some will die, and soon, I fear.
The dawn-song blares; the curtains pulse with wind;
The shutters bar the early light. How strange,
How strange it is to be alive, and back
Where I belonged so much, now not at all.

Elegy

in memoriam Jos Driver, headmaster, 1954-1965

I found the road, and then the turning right
Just past the second dam, and up the hill:
    The floating trees were there, still —
    The valley dropping down from sight.

The red-earth drive rising to the big house
Set firm in solid white against the sky:
    The school my father left, to die
    Ten days later, in a strange place.

I stopped the car to hold the moment thus,
To see the things that had or hadn't changed,
    The lawns and gardens re-arranged,
    The classrooms added to the house,

The way the trees had grown, shrinking distance.
Once, this was my home, and it isn't now.
    I turn to show my daughter how
    The shape of things has altered since.

It made me catch my breath to see the known
Unchanged, and yet I hardly knew a face;
    Strange to be a stranger in a place
    Which once had seemed so much my own.

A grave-eyed child is brought to say hullo.
I have to ask again the name I thought
      I heard, and heard all right: I taught
      Her father thirty years ago,

When mine was ill and — too briefly — I returned.
I should have stayed; instead I went away
      To where I thought my duty lay.
      You died then, when my back was turned.

I knew quite well I wouldn't see you here
But nonetheless I guess I hoped to learn
      Miraculous on my return
      That we had somehow skipped the years

And, when I'd seen the hall they built to mark
Your name and years of service here, I took
      Myself away alone to look
      At where I knew you'd be at work

If you were here at all. For sure it's you
I came to see, and really nothing else.
      In that dark house no shadow falls
      Across the threshold. That's not you

Ghostly at the desk. That's me. That damned pipe
and those long nights of sharpened pencils, soon
      And sooner took you off too young —
      And almost all that's left is hope

That we might meet on the last busy day —
If such a day there is. And I despair
    As I stare out of doors to where
    I hear the latest children play:

There is no God, there is no life to come,
There is no time when we shall meet again:
    We have to learn to live with pain,
    Impermanence, and our long home.

And as I stood in blank-eyed misery there
Reflecting on my father who was dead,
    My daughter took my arm and said,
    'I thought that I might find you here.

'You've come to look for him, I know. I told
The others where you'd be. It's just like you.
    I wish that I could meet him too.
    I want a father when I'm old.'

Well, Goodbye

I'd been skirting it all day, what I'd say
At our last parting, at the aerodrome
(Our joking way of sharing older times
To use the older terms gone out of taste).
Of course we knew. At lunch I said something
Rather feeble about the next summer —
Already I had shifted hemispheres
And meant the summer on the northern side.
Of course we knew. This was to be our last
Goodbye. There would be no more coming back.
We've always hated partings, kept them brief,
Said, 'Well, goodbye,' touched quickly, turned and
    walked —
And don't look back.
                        And don't look back. And that
Was what we did; habit saved us from grief,
At least in public. It'd been just the same
Leaving home for boarding school, the long wait
On the hot platform, parents standing there,
And nothing left to say, not even
Silly things like, 'Now don't forget to write.'
We used to say to them: 'Goodbye and go.
We're on the train leaving any moment now.
Why wait? Why drag this parting out? We don't
Want to go away — you know. Any moment now
Mom will cry. Please go. Just say goodbye.'

The night he died, before I heard the news,
I woke at three, in a far country, far
Even from England. I had a dream.
I often dreamed of him, my small brother
With cancer, though never dead. But this time
He was dead. I was sure. I woke in tears.
He'd come to me, as ghost, or something else,
To let me know, with gruff laconic words:
'So this is where you are, in India ...
I thought I'd better let you know. I'm off ...'
And then, as usual, flatly, 'Well, goodbye.'
And I woke up, in grief but also joy,
Since wordless Simon had to go like that —
And going thus meant something else than death;
And I thought: but no one will believe this —
I should wake my hosts to say, 'My brother's dead;
I know he's dead,' before they telephone —
But I can't wake them now; it's three o'clock.
I'll tell them when we meet for morning tea.
I forgot, of course. One does. The call came
At breakfast time.

———————〰〰〰◉〰〰〰———————

BASIL DU TOIT

Darwinism

How to adapt to you, how to survive in
        your searing, wispy airs,
        your post-volcanic sands,
prospering on little or on different.

I'd have to settle for roots and barks,
        drink sea fogs,
        swallow grind-stones
to churn the grass in my stomach;

engross some parts and play down others
        like a Galapagos turtle
        diverging outwards
from predator-trimmed relatives elsewhere.

To inhabit your kind of world I'll need
        poisonous spit,
        a rougher skin
and dribbling surface glands.

I'll hold thee, forsaking height and grace
        as the welwitchia does,
        sprawling in loops
like a tree with cerebral palsy.

How to breathe in your planet, without
        rasping, bug-eyed, for air.
        How to live with you —
you, who are so inhospitable to love.

Thorn Trees

Axes thud on them all day
for barricades and firewood.
The wood fractures messily, hinging itself
at the breaks with tough hempen elbows.

The bark isn't made for easily sloughing
or fissured with a menstrual heaviness;
it's fainter, more like a *trompe l'oeil* skin
applied straight onto the wood.

When summer vegetation stands high and dry,
squeaking like derelict water pumps,
and cicadas protract their skewering noise,
the thorn waits beside skulls and horns.

For a few days in spring
other trees rut with their obvious blossoms
but a fine, green lace blurs the thorn
and issues a noticeable, dry perfume.

Now goats rear cautiously against the trees,
one forefoot drooping daintily,
and twist their heads into a basket of thorns
to sample the scented needlework.

Photographing Lobatse

1
Our dignified family camera
folded out into a tapering
long-nosed accordion,
delicate, handsome, black,
like a widow
alighting from a carriage.
One serrated wheel and a small lever
at the fangled end
were its only concession
to the fickleness of natural light.
Like many a weak-chested old camera
it kept overdosing on light
through cracks
in its leathery squash-box.

A complete study of my home town
seemed a task
befitting the instrument,
so I set off like the ship's botanist
with a map and a bottle of water
and raised the neat, hinged
sighting square
of my specimen box
on the biggest meat canning factory
in the Southern Hemisphere,

year-in, year-out hill profiles,
Bella's house,
some important collections of water
and the station's flaking eucalyptuses.

The prints came back from Mafeking,
their rough heat sweetened
to a rosy, chemical light
by the lesions
in the camera's
hyper-ventilating thorax.
Peering at panoramas
from rugged hill vantages
had sapped its mechanical powers.
It dwindled the town
into the middle of its images,
sky-drowned,
earth-smothered
by too much background and foreground.

2
No record now remains
of we who lived there more naturally
than High Commissioners
or colonial traders
flogging ground-nuts
from dusty hessian sacks.
Because we were as ordinary
as our whiteness permitted,

the town's day after day
has brushed off all traces
of our domicile.
Maps confirm its radical integrity:
in its westward reaches lie
no named settlements for almost a thousand miles.

The Skull in the Mud

A security guard buzzes me in
past his trapdoor to the nation's
bibliographical honeycombs.
I pull long drawers of greasy cards
from their lettered cabinets
like the fuel rods of a nuclear reactor.
A hired scurrier, travelling
mostly on foot, carries my slip
into the immense depositories,

while I wait on my numbered chair
in the Reading Room. A leaflet explains
why this wait could last for two days.
Opposite, an advocate's aide broods
over law books as big as suitcases.
A clock twiddles my lunch hour away
but at last the steward returns,
and Livingstone's first thin pamphlet
from *Outposts* lies in front of me.

It's a far cry from apple picking
or working silver muscles of fish
out of the sea, or lifting
broodframes from their hive box
like heavy photosensitive plates.
It's not like diving to inspect
the jawbones of a new dam
or clouting a daylight owl from the sky
with a walloping boomerang.

Older Women

for Don Maclennan

The women I look to now
have already been shaped
by sexual partners. One thinks
of work-polished handles,
a sleep-slackened bed.
Their rough, plain fingers
shod with marriage iron
have fondled balls, wiped
arses, taken temperatures.
Years of withstanding
have made them tactful
surrenderers, but secretly
their gentle opinions
are bolted to concrete.

Ideas for a Research Project
in the Humanities

(a) Make a study of all the acts of love
which took place in this city on this day.
Study them like ballets
as if they had been choreographed and staged
or else study them like armed robberies
captured murkily on videotape.
Take down any dialogue.
Record their movements in an approved notation
so that students can repeat them
exactly in classroom and laboratory.
Sniff them, touch the entanglements.
Measure all departures from the classical norm.
Time them, mark them on a city map
and publish your findings —
in subsequent days men and women
will shelter in your pages,
running yellow highlighters through the abnormalities.

(b) There is a photograph of her in Tours
standing beside Wilhelm and me.
Specialise in that one second of her life
using the photograph as your source material.
Find out what she was feeling, who she loved.
What did she weigh at that moment?
(Weigh her blood separately from her bones.)

Express her total volume in fluid ounces
and number the hairs on her head.
What was that book clutched under her elbow?
Empty out her purse and list everything in it.
Transfer her psychology onto a desktop globe:
lay it out like continents
and light it from within.
List the traces of men in her — seed, spittle and
     memories.
Try to find some clue
why things ended as they did.

JOHN EPPEL

━━∿∿∿∿⊙∿∿∿∿━━

Walking Home in Early Winter

Another day passes, but before
the last light cools off the pitched housetops
of Stornaway, and the last pine door
is locked; before bedroom curtains stop
the prurient eye (this one going
grey); a moment before my right heel
takes the weight off my left toe — a ring
of smoke and a dusty song reveal,
on the corner of Weir, a 'houseboy'
with some biblical name like Thomas
or Philemon. We exchange a coy
greeting: 'Salibonani Oubaas.'
'Yebo Umfaan.' Scent of tobacco
mingles with dry grass, floor polish, beans
boiling over.

        I hear the warm glow
of his pipe being knocked to smithereens;
the scent accompanies me along
Weir Avenue; fades into beer and
braaied mealies by Flint Road; but the song,
a nocturne for Matabeleland,
stays with me, is with me still, as I
greet my family, take my wife's hand
and say: 'This is where I want to die.'

Jasmine

When they cried freedom, when the sweet
mingling of woodsmoke and jasmine
with dust: grass, granite, antelope
bone: gathered into wrists which turned

light the colour of blood, darkness
a memory of the colour
of blood — when their voices lifted
that song and sent it echoing

across Africa, I knew it.
Sibanda had taught it to me.
Polishing the family's shoes,
squatting outside the scullery

door. We both wore khaki trousers
many sizes too big; no shirt,
no shoes. I spat on the toecaps
while he brushed; and while he brushed

we sang: 'Nkosi sikelel'
iAfrika ...' over and over
till the birds joined in. August birds.
'... maluphakamiswu dumo lwayo ...'.

It comes back to me, this August,
now that the jasmine is blooming
and the air is stilled by woodsmoke;
how they cried freedom, and how I

knew their song. A lingering chill
pinches Zimbabwean sunsets
into the cheeks of my children
squatting beside me as I write.

It is their song too. I teach it
to them, over and over, till
my tired eyes are pricked with tears
held back, sweet smoke, dust, and jasmine.

Waiting for the Bus

All along the road from Bulawayo
to Gwanda or Matopos or Vic Falls;
at bus-stops, lay-bys, under shadeless trees,
the people wait beside their bundled things.
All day long they wait, and sometimes all night
too, and the next day — anxiously waiting.

Waiting for the public transport to stop
and let them in and take them home. Waiting
with babies to nurse, children to comfort
and feed, chickens, the occasional goat.
They have learnt to come prepared, with blankets,
izinduku, pots for cooking sadza.

Waiting for ZUPCO or SHU-SHINE, AJAY,
to get them to their Uncle's funeral,
their cousin's wedding, their baby brother's
baptism. Watching the new Camper Vans
cruising by. Anxious to be at work on
time. Anxious not to lose their jobs. Waiting.

They take their time now not by wrist-watches
but by the sun and the stars and the moon;
by the appearance of mopani worms;
by the ripening of marula fruit;
by the coming of the rains. Not by bus
timetables but by birth, marriage, and death.

And while they wait they count the jets that fly
to Harare and Johannesburg.
Liverish businessmen sucking whiskies
are in these jets. And Chefs with mistresses
wearing the latest digital watches.
Digital dolly-birds. All carry brief-

cases with combination locks, and next
to nothing inside: dark glasses, perhaps;
and a newspaper to study the Stock
Exchange; something digital, perhaps, for
calculating profit and ... more profit.

It's something for the people to do while
they wait — counting the jets high overhead.
Often the vapour trail is the only
cloud in the sky. No Forex for buses,
they tell us, but the five-star hotels go
up, and another Boeing is purchased.
All day they wait; all night; long-suffering.

And when, at last, a bus does stop, its tyres
are likely to be bald, its brakes likely
to be held together with wire, its body
battered, belching clouds of brain-tightening,
lung-collapsing smoke. Who's responsible?
'Not me,' says the Chef dipping his fingers

in his girl-friend's cocktail, shifting his vast
belly, vast enough to accommodate
at least seven baby goats. 'Don't look at
me,' says the Managing Director; 'my
bottom line is profit. I owe it to
the shareholders. Another whisky please?'

And don't think it's going to be any
different tomorrow or the next day
or the next. The time of sweet-becoming
is over. For those millions who depend
on buses, nothing has changed; only their
expectations have once again been dashed.

The time of bitter arrival is here:
not safe new buses, but the amassing
of personal wealth, the cultivation
of another crop of heroes. Street
names change, statues change; hotels go up, jets
go up, and the people go on waiting.

Ndebele: *izinduku* — *knobkieries*

Our Last Hot Spell

This is our last hot spell for, let me see,
a moment, two seasons, and eternity.
The haze, as thick as cotton waste, plugs
our senses. A wind stirs, a strychnos shrugs
off dying leaves; slow fruit sickens
and drops to inspire men and concuss chickens.

The late sun smears with gore our senses;
a wind stirs dislodging rust from fences
that keep out bushveld. Memories turn
like falling leaves, to smoulder and burn.
This is our last hot spell for, let me see,
a moment, two seasons, and eternity.

Strychnos spinosa: monkey orange tree

Jacaranda

Not for that Matabele the plopping
sub-resonance of Brazilian blue
blooms, as clapperless as the bell his Mum
once used to call her boy: 'Hosea, bring
checha lo second course'; which now stands sprue-
marked, missed, achromatistous, and dumb
like Ndimande, who kept a large pair
of scissors in his eyes. Not for this 'ou'
your late September flush of beautiful
violet-blue blossoms, a colour so rare,
so indescribably rare, and so, oh
so apt to rhyme with verandah. Your bull-
necked, drum-thighed Rhodesian in a powder
blue safari-suit two sizes too small;
bignonia shaped, tight forward, mauled, rucked
representative; no one is louder
when it comes to curling the lips at all
things) bright and beautiful than our product
of Plumtree, of Falcon, of Milton; our
small-but-vigorous cocked, vast bummed hero.
Not for Hosea — they'll reap the whirlwind —
Ndimande either, your 'sweep flower
off lo driveway checha'. Why must they grow
things you can't eat or smoke or sell? What kind
of Boss — stab, stab — is this who worships trees
with flowers that make work, and sting like bees?

Note: The Brazilian Jacaranda is widely planted as a street tree and in
gardens and has become naturalised in parts of Zimbabwe. As the flowers
are pollinated by bees when they've fallen to the ground, it's advisable not
to walk barefoot on them.

Dispersal

I open the Bible at random;
it not quite peels like thighs, not quite falls
like cards, but seems to waft; wafts like an
imagined aroma of seedpods —
Albizia amara I think.
There was a cluster of them in our
garden. Very old trees dying back
a bit every year. Sibanda used
their roots to make soap; I watched the sky
through their feathery leaves.

                        It is called
stichomancy: open the Bible
at random and read the first line you
see. With us it's not quite a game, not
quite spiritual guidance; rather
it's a recollection of bitter
Albizias that began dying
long after we were born, and will be
dying long after we are dead.

                        The
Bible lands open on Sibanda's
cook-boy name, Job, and I read: 'He shall
return no more to his house.' I close

the book but the smell lingers, the smell
of seedpods maturing. They'll open
in November; the seeds will be dis-
persed at random. No, it's not quite love,
and it's not quite long odds. It's the smell
of words not quite turning into trees.

SHARI EPPEL

Whale Song

I went down to the bottoms of the mountains;
the earth with her bars was about me forever
(Jonah 2,6)

I
I can remember nothing
of the world out there,
the infinite world from which
I surely came.
Some mad tide dragged me,
sucked me through the webs of time
into this dark wet place.
I am bellied in deep waters,
deeper than buried caves.
The darkness is entire,
yet it is neither still nor quiet in here.
I am cradled by her whale-sounds:
heart-beats, gurglings, wrap my head,
her rockings and shiftings encompass me.
Her sea-currents wash me
through and through.
I am chained to her, it seems,
yet kindly so. She feeds me
and I grow.
I grow and grow.

II
He stirs in me,
deeper than thought:
it is the beginning of something,
a sentence we will live out together.
He is trapped in my sea-cave,
bound to its nurturing wall.
Yet who is captive to whom?
The answer is not at all clear.

He grows and grows,
expanding his niche,
elbowing me aside.
A fearful wonder he is,
this hanger-on,
this free-riding Jonah of mine.
He will beach me.

III
How did I come here?
Still I remember nothing.
This closeness is intense,
unbearably so:
if I move a fraction, or hiccup,
she will know.

This bondage is enough.
Surely, I have served my time.
There's a world out there —
did I know it once? —
it calls me from this cove.

IV
At night with unshut eyes
we gaze through darknesses,
we dream and dream
of the coming
of the birth-tide.

V
It is here — we are glad:
we surf the pain,
traverse the peaks of fear.
We will soon be freed
from this now belly of hell.

She cries out, calls my name.
She is delivered,
she delivers me
upon the dry land.

Vigil for R.K.C.,
Dying of Anorexia Nervosa

My tears have been my meat day and night,
while they continually say unto me, Where is thy
God? (Psalm 42)

I dream I am newborn
sucking and pulling at your breast,
Mother.
With my hungry mouth
I chew, gulping warm milk.
Gnawing and mashing
I eat you up —
your milk, the tender rawness
of your torn nipples: their taste,
the smell of your blood as familiar
as my first breath.
Unforgiving, I eat you, I eat you
but you are always there:
the wet crescent darknesses
of your watching eyes
the huge warmth
of your breast, blood, milk,
from the beginnings
of time, my mother.

My emaciated lord, my love —
you, too, gaze me down.
I kneel before you, openhearted,
but your outstretched, transfixed
arms cannot enfold me in a hug.
Your funeral eyes ford depths
unknown to me.
You have mastered suffering:
your hands, your feet are bloodied,
your side gushing.
I have much to learn from you.
Such beauty in your sunken ribs.
I strive to emulate you,
your still, near-death pose:
but I can never be thin
enough to please:

I am bloated with needs.

And so, you two keep watch,
vigilant eyes full
of love and hate and fear
imploring me:
eat; live; eat.
But I spit you out, mother, lord,
all of you.

I will conduct my own death watch.

────◅◦▸────

FRANCIS FALLER

Taking Stock in May

Now: the first hints of harsh, brittle winter:
a thin bed of soil on the window-pane;
the yard's warmth, the grass's heavy green
hauled aloft on the squawks of migrant cranes;
all that's lush crushed by stamping feet;
the sun, its tank of gas deplete,
heading north to find a pump across the border.

Now the salaams of swallows.
They swoop and scrape the ground
in specious shows of loyalty,
and clouds in tatty grey
rehearse a final gig,
nostalgic for those summer days
when drumming and twanging on the roof
got thunderous applause.
Now it's time to take the road,
when pods on the creeper
crackle and explode, and seeds slip
into envelopes addressed to spring.

Now the stream is all rock,
supermarket trolley, empty lager can;
heaps of rubbish puff their pipes
and, stripped of their disguise,
thorns and razor-wire proliferate,
sharpening the bark of dogs.
Now gloves and scarf — stuffed away in shelves —
flutter to life, the last of the moths.
Things we'd put away for good return:
the number of our years, the TB coughs.

Now a barbet brings desperate news:
days are running like a nose with cold.
And now the houses: life-long wondercoat
suddenly
is old.

A Note About Spring

When all the array of colours collapsed
into a rubble of sepia nonentity,
we found winter wreckage at our feet
and, in our boles, a skein of cracks.

We hardly knew, then,
the bare economy of love,
the way it copies solid wood:
dropping all protection;
to the first foray of frost
falling naked in defence.
Hence the meticulous wind
sweeping fragments of a lusher life
into a pile, into the rubbish bin.

Now again spring unfurls.
Welcome to this strangely warmer world.
Welcome to the strength we learnt:
to live in monochrome, drab and thin,
to concentrate our power on the inner ring.
All this time our roots have tunnelled into rock;
above, little bombs notching up the days.
And just a few erratic flames
set our seared, sapped energy ablaze.

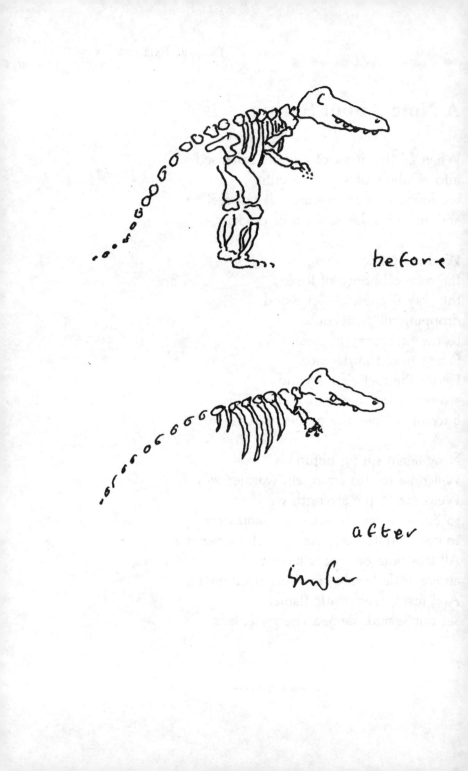

before

after

GUS FERGUSON

―――――――

Poetry at the Whale-Well

13 November 1994

The skeletons of floating whales,
suspended from the roof —
hindquarters gone completely
from the pelvis to the hoof.

Their little, ineffectual arms
that dangle at each side
suggest to us their mothers were
prescribed Thalidomide.

This causes me to speculate,
while poets read their verse,
that Darwin's climb from sea to land
went, sometimes, in reverse.

Perhaps an ozone crisis let,
in years and years gone by,
mutational radiation stream
unhindered through the sky.

This sparked a great variety
of new genetic forms,
though many species went extinct,
or had to shift their norms.

There was a group of herbivores
that roamed the littoral zone,
they were as large as dinosaurs
but mammals to the bone.

And when the cataclysm came,
millennia ago,
these lumbering vegetarians
were dealt a cruel blow —

Their young were born with withered arms,
completely without legs
and lumped around like giant slugs
or rolled about like kegs.

They were dehydrating quickly
beneath the savage sun
when adults came and nudged them
in the water, one by one.

They flopped and flapped in shallow waves
and found that they could swim
(In ocean as in amnion,
they had no need of limb).

So, buoyant in the surging surf
they mewled their sad goodbyes,
and still today, the sea resounds
with deeply plaintive cries.

This might explain why many die
when stranded by the tide.
Oh, could it be nostalgia drives
the whales' mass suicide?

Gale Warning

The papaya tree
Flaps in the wind
Taps windows
And rattles the eaves:

Flags for the deaf
And morse for the blind, it signals
With snail-tattered leaves.

Tanka

Each shrub has roots
Up in the sky the clouds move.
We are growing old,
And yet and yet each moment
Is total and eternal.

Midlife Crisis
Or Plato's Cave again revisited

Transfixed, I stand upon the stair
at work and watch, reflected in the
foyer mirror, etched silhouettes
of children, shadowed on a sun-
bleached wall, careering off to school.

JEREMY GORDIN

Kaddish
E.G., 1911-1989

God of my Fathers, that's all You are:
the god of some bearded Hebrew ancients
clustered near a tent in the Sinai sand.
I don't believe in You, nor did my father.

Yet how You would always lurk close by him:
in his jokes, his Yiddish, his enchantment
as he pored over another Talmudic commentary
having set the sprinkler in the sunlit garden.

Now I must leave him in a box in the earth
while the sun blazes and a cemetery sprinkler
ticks round and round like a crazed clock.

God of my Fathers, Blessed be Thy Name,
I don't believe in You, nor did my father.
Yet always lurk, I beseech You, close by him.

Name

Could be the original was something else entirely,
'Gordin' merely a loan to avoid military service ...
Who'll ever know? Hitler's men marched on Latvia
and the records, along with the people, became smoke.

And where'd 'Gordin' come from anyway?
Insane Baron Gordon the convert?
The city of Grodno? What about
that 'i'? Did my grandfather write too fast,

truncating 'vav' into 'yud'? I'll stick
with the old way, which is more precise: I am
Yeremiyahu ben Eliyahu, Jeremy the son of Elias.

For though neither of us turned out a prophet
or even holy, we remain, unquestionably,
father and son, son and father.

STEPHEN GRAY

Returnees

on their knees touch soil
a generation lost and found

frame time again and
focus on the true subject

bring expertise and vocabulary
from another world apart

apply themselves to pulling closed
the chasm between their and our lives

the great rift will soon entomb
their and our past, level all

renegotiating exile they face
privately the force of their desertion.

Slaughtered Saints

a row of graves in the veld, bar-code of death
at Sharpeville again — black coffins before
a soccer stadium of mourners —

this recurs as the great South African ceremony:
public weeping, no compensation, together
only in the mass shuffle of their united end

what then, once the chants and sermons are done,
the bodycount of liberation, the victims
guilty of their innocence, their reduction to dust?

who worked out how many it takes?
do they signify, either way?
— did anyone consult with *them*? —

the late martyrs of Boipatong — mother and babe
elbow to elbow in the winter grit — able-bodied
certainly had other hopes of their different lives —

and if they said they wished to speak to us
what then? and who would listen?
what would we offer in return for their few, honest
    words?

would they then set about to kill their killers?
mass with sticks and stones their dreadful regret,
rampage against their lack of fortune?

take by the throat the privileged few,
scoop from the mouths of others' children
a spoonful of porridge, a nub of meat on the bone?

this early death hath only made them hungry
for the life they never had: girlfriends,
fast cars, for shopping from huge supermarkets

and the greedy needs of the dead do not end:
they want impossibly: music and song,
they want padding and waterproof, comforts

next thing they'll want mod cons,
to watch themselves on TV getting mown down
by private armies, presidents of all

parties and denominations come to mourn them;
what they'll next demand is bullets
(just wait!) and their own rolled razor-wire,

keep the predators out, flowers on their tombs ...
but no one asks the blood and ashes, nor ever will.
what would happen then would only overkill ...

don't anyone consult with them; bury them,
the lonely martyrs of Boipatong,
lest the slaughtered saints recur, recur.

The Herb Garden

My mother before she died insisted
I should have a herb garden
Something in her English soul
Amid rough South Africans
Called for the tenderness of mint
The old scent of lavender and sage

They arrived in soggy pages of *The Star*
With a spade taller than herself
She dug them into my backyard
Before I was ready for them
A cigarette tightly in her lips
Explaining chives made life worthwhile

That is how she died in her own
Garden of sweet remembrance
Very frail then with a bucket and spade
The size we children used for play
Always finding the sun too hot the soil
Far too dry for the gentler herbs

Today after the long heart-stopping drought
My mother's bed of lost spices
Has so flourished I have cut it back
And the mint is in the crevices of fingers
The sage under my very nails
And I remember her every gesture.

MICHAEL CAWOOD GREEN

Falling (Hettie's Love Song)

Oosthuizen, Hester C., gebore van der Watt:
10.4.1930 — 3.8.1964

> *For Esthie — who should have been called,*
> *after her maternal grandmother, Hester*

I thought it was the sea
Dragging me to the surface,
And away from you;
By the time I began to swim to consciousness
(Registering at some level
That our beach holiday was over,
The shore two days,
An unresolved argument, and
Hundreds of solid earth miles
Away)
I had no way of comprehending
This new reality;
Such fluidity in a foundation
I, a mine worker's wife, after all,
Have often known to dance
Only made sense within the logic
Of the ocean;
Here, though, no lift first
From a rising swell —
Only the drop,

A falling away from the norm, the base, the limit,
The support and measure of all
I know — even the sea,
The crumpled, deathless sea,
Where *the water takes my body without shame,*
And my children dive
To surface again scared and laughing,
And you are always there
To catch me.

I had time,
Moving through the roar like waves,
To untangle myself from you and
Step from our bed,
Fight the floor for purchase
With no legs for this changing element,
And reach a buckling wall,
Where the light switch briefly obeyed
Laws we command by
Submitting ourselves to them;
Blinded at first by the yellow flood
The firm lines of familiarity flickered through into focus
Only to blur quickly into their collapse
When gravity became the only certainty,
Our children a lost hope in another room,
And I heard myself fill the space
Falling away beneath my feet with screaming
As I tried to find my way across all eternity

Back to you.

A Washing Machine at the End of the World

Nothing of importance occurred here, and nothing much of interest, for everybody was wealthy and flourishing. Lady Anne Barnard, Journal of a Tour into the Interior, *1798.*

Several of the photographic spreads
Covering Blyvooruitzicht's overnight sensation
Feature it:
A washing machine
Poised inches from the edge of the half-house
Not taken by the 'sinkholegrave'
Which swallowed whole three others,
One complete with a family of five.

This is no subject for the romantic gesture,
Where the earth now, say, like Pringle's sea once,
'Howls for the progeny she nurst,
To swallow them again';
Neither is it cool-blue modern urban stuff
Of Unreal Cities and, say, the buried blooming.
No, this is the place where Viv's *'Wonderful'*
(*'My nerves are bad to-night. Yes, bad'*)
Becomes Ezra's *'Photography?'*,
Where the camera captures a cross-section
Of the ordinary.
The surgery of catastrophe strips away
The invisibility of the familiar,
And the home dissected reveals

For social analysis
The square, enamelled, churning heart
Of our domestic fantasies.

This is why,
Despite Lady Anne's epitaph
For the whole history
Of the middle class,
A family of five
In a hole interests us far more
Than a crusher-crew of twenty nine
Or any number of other more spectacular
Displays of disaster
Involving soldiers, sailors,
Policemen, firemen —
                    Workers . . .

It's that damn washing machine that worries us,
So similar to the ones nestled
In our own kitchens or laundries,
Solid consumers of our soiling natures,
Safe as houses.

The Big Picture

*I said, 'Graham, what on earth do you think they'll call it in
history?' and he said, 'I've just read a book that refers to ours
as the Late Bourgeois World. How does that appeal to you?'*
Nadine Gordimer, The Late Bourgeois World, *1966.*

The big picture,
So Dan will tell you,
Was the creation of a middle-class;
Nationalism, it seems,
For the Afrikaner,
Was *Ons Eerste Volksbank,*
Volkskas and *Uniewinkels,*
SANTAM and SANLAM — and, of course,
Federale Volksbeleggings,
Our way into the superstructures
Of mining.

For Johannes Oosthuizen,
It was the *Reddingsdaadbond,*
A trade, employment, insurance,
All woven into song and dance
In Afrikaans —
But you who have seen what the
Nationalists would give away:
The song, the dance, the pure white Afrikaans,
Leaving naked and stark
Property that's private,

Interests invested —
You can ask now,
What cost, a bourgeoisie?

Endless images
From forty lost years:
Lorries with domestic loads heading quite deliberately
    nowhere,
Workers less than the machines they operate,
Scattered bodies at odd angles in the dust,
Children's bellies pregnant with emptiness,
Bullets in a blackboard,
Screams echoing in clinical rooms ...

... even a house,
An ordinary, middle-class house,
Disappearing down a hole ...

Yes, you can ask now,
What cost, a bourgeoisie?

Failures with Metaphor

... truths are illusions of which one has forgotten that this is what they are; metaphors which have become worn out and have lost their sensual power. Friedrich Nietzsche, Ecce Homo: How One Becomes What One Is.

TAKE 1: 1972

My mind is like a midnight subway;
Your memory is the tramp
Sleeping in the corner.

TAKE 2: 1979

My mind a subway
At midnight;
The memory of you
Sleeps in the corner.

TAKE 3: 1993

Mind a subway at midnight;
Memory sleeps in the corner.

These poems are taken from *Sinking*, the story, in verse, of events which took place on 3 August 1964 at the Blyvooruitzicht Mine, Far West Rand. A.B.A. Brink, in his *Engineering Geology of Southern Africa: The First 2 000 Million Years of Geological Time*, describes what happened succinctly: 'A sinkhole appeared in a mining village in the middle of the night and claimed the lives of the Oosthuizen family of five as their house suddenly dropped more than 30 metres. Three other houses which were situated on the edge of the initial collapse also fell in within a short period of time as the sides of the sinkhole caved in, their occupants making dramatic escapes. Subsequent enquiry revealed that there had been leakage from water pipes in the area where the sinkhole appeared.'

Sinking attempts to fill out this textbook account from a number of different perspectives.

JAMES A. HARRISON

Homecoming

Suspended between worlds in departures, beyond
    security,
not yet out but forbidden to turn back,
one hovers in a shiny space filled with things to sit on.
The journey itself uneventful, even tedious,
lacks all sensation of travel, of flying the length unseen
of a continent and the width of the widest sea,
or approaching an island, uncommonly green.

Heathrow is huge and hurrying, yet orderly, even
    reassuring.
The shuttle bus driver knew and liked my country.
Driving a tiny Volkswagen on the usual left,
I found the M4 without difficulty. More cars, more trucks
but unmistakably a freeway, familiar if not tame
— even the signs were colour correct.
I drove towards Bristol as if it were Bloemfontein.

The English countryside is green, green upon green and
    leafy,
like illustrated nursery rhymes and the pictures in story
    books,

or like desired results in gardening magazines.
There are buildings older than the colonies; they breathe
the atmospheres of cherished literature, of history
I learned in school. And everyone spoke my language,
with irritating accents but without mystery.

It was not novelty but familiarity that disturbed,
like the shock of *déjà vu*. A hemisphere from home,
nevertheless, at home, because home is the place
of understood meanings, where the worth and weight
of things are granted and customs go unquestioned.
One goes unnoticed there because one has always been
    there.
A member of the family, I was camouflaged and bland.

Returning to this hybrid culture, it was strange to feel
again not embedded but precarious, dangling on the
    fringe.
Meadows and the Queen's English are deep and dear,
as owned as Afrikaans and koppies in dry landscapes,
but I am no colonist, no matter how those winds blow.
Living without a tribe is insecure, lonely;
the homefires burn low.

The Visit

Sneaking down the passage
I grinned in anticipation
of the fright I would give
my little boy as I sprang
roaring into the room.

Inside there was no son
but my father, tall and well.
Saying nothing he smiled
and tickled me till I woke,
wondering at the trickery

of my dreaming subconscious mind.
Then I cried to realise
that my father, six months dead
and gone, had just paid me
a brief but friendly visit.

EVELYN HOLTZHAUSEN

The Voyeur

This attitude of woman, freshly showered,
towelled dry, windmills
up an arm, applies a hiss of spray,
winds down, turns the other way.

The sight of surface nakedness,
voluptuous flesh, breasts,
the tuft of pubic hair:
A voyeur's vignette, indifferent to my stare.

Frantic gusts of winter wind whip
shards of rain to scratch
against the window pane:
Excite suburban lawns to erupt in flood.

She folds down, snakes into a dress
shrugs, reaches back
to seal a mesh of zip,
then strides, preoccupied, into the next room.

A scented spice of woman lingers in the air,
and seems to carry insinuation,
as vague as loss, like water
permeates a film of wet this side of cold glass.

CHRISTOPHER HOPE

Heat

Listen, can you hear the music? In the room
next door they're playing Schubert. The piano
keeps falling downstairs, the strings
sound amused. The neighbours below are cooking
mascara stew. It's their special of the day;
they eat it when they're sad. Someone says
it's because they're Iranian but I don't buy that.
The piano is on its feet again, and dancing,
the strings are leading, showing the way
across the sunny floors of Austrian streams
where tickled trout are dreaming that this
is how it would be if rainbows could swim.
Now the piano is giving a little sermon
and the violins are trying not to laugh.
My neighbours' cooking punches through
the floorboards. There is too much garlic
in that mascara, but then there always is.

And you are in your garden, somewhere in Africa,
jumping the trampoline. I hear the steady
tragic note as your heels hit rubber,
the triple echo of protesting springs.
The neighbours see only your head, its helmet
of red hair, round as a penny, trying to push

its way into heaven. Like a gambler feeding
a fruit machine. You're planning to keep
doing this until you go broke, or win ...
and every spin keeps coming up cherries.
Ah, but the sun sees what the neighbours
miss. You're naked as the drought-struck Namib,
as dry-boned Eritrea, burning everywhere.

Rumour speaks well of your several lives:
the belly-dancing; three freckled kids;
of a ghost who hangs around you, careful
with his cuffs, smooth as a coin.
Your news reaches me on paper napkins, pages
torn from reporters' notepads, on wires singing
inside my head. So *this* is the cottage
where the thieves broke in? This the ring-pull
from the can of Coke your grandmother wore,
jewelry for dying in. Your hot terrain,
remote as Rangoon, boils and sings.
Here it is winter. Big black nights
muscle in like bailiff's men, punishing
unwise investments in the southern sun.
My neighbours are cooking fish tonight.
It's Friday. Side by side in the oven,
pursed in cooking foil, two trout pinken
in scalding steam. I close my eyes.
Next door the music begins again. Violins,
piano pressing black fingers to its pale lips.
I'm searching for something I cannot see.
Will you tell me when I'm getting warm?

Unrest Report of a Father

Here
at this corner
they shot my son

he was seventeen
he had dropped out of school
the situation was not such
that he could study, he said

he couldn't allow his comrades to die
while he was reading Shakespeare

Of course I did not approve

when he fired rubber tyres
and waved a red flag
flaming across the street
in front of the garage:
just think of the fire hazard

My shop is just around the corner
and while he still came home
he got a hiding every night
but it didn't help

In the end I gave up
I didn't even know
where he was hiding out

And then they shot him
here at this street corner
not far from my shop

A Court Case

The district attorney
kicked a skull
under the table of the judge
and shouted goal
he was later crowned
sportsman of the year
by the state president

The witnesses for the defence
could only remember
that a murderer
who had steamed a worker alive
was given a suspended sentence
and that a farmer
who had poured boiling water
down the throat of one of his farm workers
got off scot free

One advocate quoted long passages
from the *One Hundred Days of Sodom*
to prove the innocence
of the average South African reader in general
and the accused in particular

The judge was determined

After studying the case for twenty-four hours
he didn't understand anything
but unfolded his aching limbs
and opened the door
and waiting for the advocates
threw them down the staircase
shouting: cockroaches!

He then painted his face orange, white and blue,
took off all his clothes
and entered the courtroom.

Before he could be prevented
by the panicking advocates
he pronounced the verdict:
guilty.

No appeal.

Later the judge was braaied
on a spit
together with a three-legged giraffe
and was entered into
the Guinness Book of Records

For Vukin Before Your Birth

Now to satisfy being made
for love and love-making
creators with muscle and bone

we have created you
out of our pearl-eruption
orgasmic flower
and every flower buds to blossom
to brilliant

sun-shine

though there is no inkling
how you will manifest
our child for whom we wait

each turn in the belly
brushing
we lie together
extolling the womb-universe
caress you mutually
to combine and instil
the sap, the spring, the serene
bow you will need to shape

you will pierce
the veil of water
wherein you turn
to verify the air of earth

we flank you now
and so long
as we have breath

ALAN JAMES

~~~~~~~~~⦿~~~~~~~~~

Cape St Francis: Then and Now

Once, in my boyhood, there
was no apparent ugliness, not
here, not that I could
see: but I was young,
almost innocent, unaware of the
deeper theology of the landscape.
I look back at it
now: the humped sand with
dune thickets, the sea quarrie,
blue kunjibush, the kooboo berry,
potato creepers and monkey ropes,
low, gnarled, pruned by stiff
successive air: there the bushbuck,
the duiker took cover, found
food, browsed on fruits, roots,
tubers: there the bulbuls, speckled
mousebirds, seedeaters: virtually unpeopled:
and one had to go
by landrover to get through
the loose tracks over the
covered dunes to where one
wanted to be, and when
one arrived there was little
that had been added — the

tower, yes, and its adjacent
support buildings: nothing else subverted
the unskinned land now turned
to account: and that turning
making apparent the blame of
the land, or to put
it another way, comprising an
elicitation of the fruits of
an inheritance that cannot but
be adiated: hard homes that
are spreading closed, sullen, as
if they can scarcely bear
the wind or each other,
or their own designs that
stump, block the brows of
sand and scrub, or tolerate
their very contents: the buttoned
cushions, wagon-wheel dining suites,
pictures of azure mountains or
sailing ships, the white appliances,
the things of brass and polished.
Take a stroll if you
like: this windswept road: its
homes strong with slasto and
breezeblocks and apertures that glare,
that squint at seeming vacancies
of sea, sky: the lawns
bristling as though contemplation of
them were trespass: a boat
in a driveway: an umbrella
on a stoep: a door

that is open, and through
it the family furniture, futile,
destructive even: and there's a
woman in the doorway: she's
holding a cup in her
hand and there is a
brown dog at her feet
in the sunlight. But you
don't speak to her. She
watches as you pass. And
then you get to a
corner and turn down to
the parking lot that gives
access to the beach and
there's a surfer waiting and
there's nobody else. Such apartness.
So little understanding. So much
disfigurement that is borne and
that has to be tolerated.

On a Track in the Backveld

The telling. Distance being dominant,
horizontality, and blankness virtually: a
concurrence of dunes, pans, waterless
courses and crumbled hills and
kraalbos and stones as stars
and dry sun that hardly
stops day by day after
day intensely and in places
the overburden is gone, the
fundament of rock being exposed
and plates of granite that
lie available for attention and
are seamed, holed, layering they
break as fired clay so
unprofitably, and a lizard bides,
blue-headed, has to, or
an ash-grey karroo rat
or sand snake with dorsal
speckling whose diet consists mainly
of lizards and rats, or
even a klipspringer, dappled, not
moving, its nose glistens, scents
the facts: a concurrence and,
you could say, a coinherence
with little change and very
scrupulous exchange, the margins slim,
options excluded, contracts long established,
tightly written: what you might

call an obstinate economy, not
open, not accommodating, not disburdened
and having no consolation to
speak of: a heartland, minimalist
country that's all taken down
to brown and near-brown,
reduction that leaves no fat,
no sweat, with a protraction
and with repetition and with
meagre deviations within strict limits,
controlled confines: layers, parts, erosions
burned dark but also lighter
browns, bronzes, tawny, and with
light slipping the paleness of
khaki and the paleness of
grey: layers and parts and
erosions, time gone and the
consequences infinitely various of motion
over time and the 'almost
solid stillness' that Conrad refers
to in *Nostromo* and the
solitude of inevitability that is
ineluctable and inscrutable and implacable —
such being the sort of
words he liked to use.
Yes, to be here, and
to consider the fact of
being here, and the heartache
of that, and of all
manner of speaking and waiting.

Cape St Francis:
A Visit Prior To Emigration

To revert. That's where
my grandfather once poked
about at shells: it
was a wintry day:
he was wearing a
heavy overcoat: his gait
was unsteady: he found
nothing he fancied: and
as it turned out,
that was his last
attendance here. Further on
is the scrum of
rocks where my dad
sometimes fished when the
water was right — not
too clear, not too
strong — there are favourable
gullies there where in
the light turbulence one
might take a plump
galjoen, or in water
a little turbid, a
kob, or, most highly
prized, a musselcracker or
even a red steenbras:
but now his tackle
is laid up and

he talks of selling
it. And somewhere up
towards Oyster Bay is
the site of a
family picnic and there
a six-pack of
Castle, left to cool
in shaded water, was
lost to the coursing
green, cold and white.
There's so much, everything
to remember, confess, own.
Yes, there are places
of intervention here that
my sentiment sanctifies as
places of belonging and
that I keep constructing:
that is how it
is and I think
that that is how
it's supposed to be —
is there another way? —
that time and place
be dealt with, with
creative reverence. So now,
finding that I must
go, I confront this
moment of departure at
this site: a farewell,
yes it is goodbye
after many arrivals, interruptions:

it has been a
long visit such that
your bush is in
my blood, the whoop
and fuss of your
birds occupy my silences:
you have kept me
as your waves, one
after another, that club
at the rocks, beat
the sand, giving themselves:
permission, grace, constantly supplied
against all odds. Now
I turn to go,
and as I turn
I ask you to
let me go that
I might be unclasped,
not an abandonment but
a sending, and a
release from anger that
I should have to
leave my possession, and
from sorrow of leaving.
A last visit but
I know there will
be others of a
sort, that I shall
face you again but,
for now this is
goodbye. My eyes shall

be awake for your
promise. You shall
be my locus and light,
and still my keep.

Memories From Childhood

That's me
in the cot.
Soft blanket across my nose.
(It became a habit: My aah;
Blue dusters, eventually.)
That's my mother,
Bending over.
You can see her lovely young body
Through the nightie;
Still lovely after five babies.
And there's Robert at two,
gazing through the struts
(I suppose I was asleep).

That's me
at three
Walking with my mum.
See that hat?
She pulled it down
To keep my big ears warm.
She's smiling at my father
And beautiful, always.
Big coat and thin jeans
(English winters).

That's me,
at five.
Cotton dress with bambi buttons,
Holding our kitten.
Mummy took this one
In Port Elizabeth.
I wasn't posing
(I never do, for her).
She made the dress, though.
The bambi buttons:
What a wonderful touch!

That's me
in my new school uniform
Holding my little tooth
Triumphantly between gripping fingers.
What an awful grin!
My father took me out
Onto the lawn
And had me smile wide enough
To show where it had come out.
(I wonder what he was doing home
During the day.)

That's me
At the beach
in a hand-me-down costume I loved
Pink floral nylon: Ugh!
Disproportionately long legs,

Like a little plump heron.
I cut this one out
For a Christmas present plate.
The picture was in the middle
And I wrote a circular love letter,
with decorations,
to Mummy,
in crayons.
She put it up
In the living room for years,
Until the dust and sun
Wore down the colours.

That's me.
Standard two:
Two plaits
Like my mother used to wear.
Mielie teeth and freckly nose.
My grandma cried
When she saw it, in England.
It reminded her
of Mummy when
She was little.

That's me.
Member of the netball team.
Gangly and naughty.
Me and my friend,
Sandra Cragg.

There aren't many of me
at primary school.
I suppose he took the camera
When he left.

⸺⁓⁓⁓ᴘ◉ᴘ⁓⁓⁓⸺

RUSTUM KOZAIN

Family Portrait

Aunt May sways, rocks herself like a baby,
chafing her heart over worn linoleum, amongst
unhinged doors resting on the floor, shrinking
in the corner of my Ma's small kitchen.

She lives there now. Her husband imported
the latest lover, keeps her, with arrears
for buildings and new cars piling up.

Brother and cousin've bought guns
making babies with one eye open on
the back door. Old enough to afford it,
they are finally prepared, and wait
for a 20 year old black onslaught.

Buckie and Mo are doped on mandrax.
Buckie robbed a bottle store, implicated
in his friend's suicide note. He still
drives the neighbourhood, waving at passersby.

Gail and her husband, two children strong,
still want to finish their studies; they
mention this everytime I wipe braaivleis juice
from the corners of my sardonic mouth.

Sonny's a principal carrying flattened joints
in his file, spinning out to a house empty
but for fishtanks, dogturds, a double mattress
and a friend's wife now his lover.

I've switched off, into loneliness
and light candles to this amber mood
driving drugs and loud music into me
dancing with my shadow bent into
the corners and ceilings of this room.

Ma says she's switched off too, can't
take the strain of everyone's problem
as the family close their eyes and stroke
their lashes according to the latest fashion.

The blood thicker than water runs thin
now holding our broken togetherness
all of us flung away from poverty.

DOUGLAS LIVINGSTONE

The Wall Beyond Station X

1

The promenade along this sunbright bank
is pleasant: folk amble; engage in talk
at tables beneath the trees; or recline
upon the springy turf, intent on love.
You stumble on it inadvertently:
a wall, two bricks wide, about two hands high
above the shallows, stretching out across
the placid surface, angled from the shore.
The wall points straightly to some promised land.
The waters on the left float one plume from
a seagull's wing; a goose-quill on the right.
Caprice? Bravado? Curiosity?
— you start along the wall: it looks quite safe.
There is something you foolishly forgot.

2

The history of walls is not too good.
Still — seabed visible, the sun above,
what little wind there is directionless —
you stride along. Hours pass. You pause, look back:

you have not reached halfway. Small puffs of cloud
have graced the sky. The wind starts gusting up
from this side first, then that. The seas appear
to darken by the now inconstant sun.
A piece of paper on the left-hand side
bears writing: formulae or diagrams.
You march on, challenged by that distant shore.
No longer can you see down through the depths:
the seas on either hand have turned opaque.
You are resolved this isthmus must be walked.

3

The sky turns overcast. You soldier on,
your journey's end in sight as ranks of reeds
— mysteriously silver — spread. The wall
cleaves through them. Then, you are in among them.
They rustle slightly, taller than a man.
All visible horizons have drawn in:
the wall knifes through. Of course, you wonder if
your present course is wise; and so you stop
a vertiginous moment when you ask
which is forward, which is back? You decide
to plod on for the reeds are thinning out.
The surface of the waters just below
has dropped: is the wall increasing in height?
You sight along it carefully, half-crouched.

4

The top is flat. Both seas appear to flow
— like time — moving forwards to one point.

Ahead, some thing is draped across the wall:
a python, its head down left, tail down right.
You near it stealthily: it is no snake
but a corpus of cables intertwined;
among them thread multihued finer wires;
a smell of ozone; occasionally
a spark. The coils bunch higher than your knee
— they look dangerously electrical.
You step across hesitantly, with care.
The reeds have gone, the waters surging swift
and rougher, so much further underfoot.
Erratic crosswinds rock and buffet you.

5

The wall narrows to one brick wide: its haft
spears blackness. You have travelled much too far
to return. You are fearfully exposed.
Far beneath, the waters churn, race ahead.
The gales strike, threatening to topple you:
torn tatters of melody from one side,
their strident voices screaming opposite
— the words incoherent. At times, both meld
in manic songs of dissonance and loss.
Little light remains: the seas have almost
vanished, but you can hear them rage — each side
spurs its vaulting wind. Equilibrium
at risk, you try a quick glance back:
the wall behind you is dissolving as you pass.

MOIRA LOVELL

Coming Home

Lugging a dead holiday in cases
We descend to the London Underground
And ride a short subterranean route
In the company of Hell's denizens
Who — six-foot-tight in skin and leather — take
Their women as they take their newspapers:
Out of the gutter and in headline style.
But from Heathrow it's celestial stuff —
God's in the cockpit; angels in the aisles
Distribute glasses of wine on the wing.
Star-scrubbed and shining we're wrapped up in clouds
While the moon is changing shifts with the sun.
Finally we are dropped out of the sky
Test old ground tentatively with new feet
And try to exhume the holiday corpse.

ROD MACKENZIE

From Cecilia Forest

Time to listen again: leaves, like the quiet smoke
Of his thought, lift free from a clearing between pines.
The tall shafts wade under the faintly printed stars —
Each blue flint forms what they are, for words and signs,
    steeped
In memory, were forged to contain and make them
Less and more than real. And so, surreal, they still reach
Into the heart of stones, leaves, twigs, and his fingers,
Twined in thought in stream and soil. Crouched, he
    relaxes
In listening harder, breathing even softer.
All the day's din fades. Distilled, the whiteness cradled
In lungs flushes through his mouth and nostrils over
The valley below, the city's toybox of blocks
Scattered across the basin to the flats. Beyond,
The thatched mountains, purpled in a shimmer of wind
And mist, lie haystacked at the edge of everything
A child could wish to believe can be, with no words
Tempered or filigreed for any other thing.
Then, there were just the sounds a six-year-old would
    spill,
Words doing the same jostling, simple chores — trusty
Buckets which clanked to and from a stream of water

Which looped to this bend in a forest, steadily
Founting through the old space where listening began.

Mother

I thought of your smile, your laugh
And touch today, when I saw
Pigeons scatter, pulsating
Through the heated fragrance
Of pine-needles. The air
Vibrated with wings.
Once I thought of your chuckle,
When a pebble clapped
A mountain pool's mirror, its sheen
Suddenly electric. The stone dropped
Like your shy, warm glance.

But none were you.
Now, as the afternoon suffuses
A vase in the room's corner
With leaf and blossom, I think
Of the lives which bloomed
Through you, which have come
And gone. What's left is a son.
What you are is this quiet.
— It's the space needed most, healing
Into being these petals and stalks,
Filaments and angles of light.

DON MACLENNAN

Letter in a Bottle

When death takes me
I'll be in no mood to recount
the way I saw things
or work out my account.
All I've ever wanted to make —
a few clean statements
on love and death,
things you cannot fake.

Letters

In his old age my father
managed to make his writing
flow like water,
ripples across a paper lake
pierced with upright stakes.
I could read waves then,
so it was not hard to follow.
Now mine begins to look the same,
but the waves run off the page
mocking my inability
to contain my age.

My father's letters look
like frozen lakes,
stiff unyielding waves,
hungry cormorants
perched on frosty stakes —
words lock-jawed
waiting for the thaw.

Summer is outrageous:
northern swallows,
fields of waist-high grass,
a moon of burning sulphur
above sandstone hills.

And writing?
Flinging words
against the world,
to conjure up the sound
and smell of things
that are themselves.

To Geoffrey

Midday on the patio:
salad and hot rolls,
coffee and cheese —
one of those winter days
that dries out into crumbs
the fallen leaves
and forces you to wear
dark glasses.

Temptation does not lie so quiet
when someone beautiful
admires your work —
this bright young girl,
complex as Aphrodite,
for example.

I am more easily satisfied:
a good lunch and a cigarette,
a glass of wine,
a friend whose conversation's
near perfect;
and sleep then, in my chair,
savouring the richness
of some paragraph.

Real temptation lies
in reading something new,
hoping to find the answer
when I should be working harder
on those things of mine
already in my hands,
and make them shine.

I look to older women now:
they are more knowing,
much kinder,
more forgiving.

Prospect

Viewed from my top-floor balcony,
bridge of a docked ship,
the red-tiled quad is empty,
washed with sun
and lunchtime quiet.
Solitary students cross the square,
ducking the budding trees
as though the space and light
were hazardous.
They walk quickly
through the glare.
Pigeons' lazy bubbling
fills the vacant hour.
Everything succumbs to noon:
north-west above the hospital
floats a thin, oxidized moon.

Behind me in my room,
the fading blue calligraphy
of lectures half-forgotten
filed and foldered in the cabinet
keeps pointless order.
There is no place to store
the fragments that I prize —
not even my head
is the right size.
But out here on the balcony
I repossess

the privilege of silence,
imagining what was possible,
and everything that might be.
I have outlived my intellect —
washed up on a vacant beach,
watching, listening
in the emptied day.

Warm wind flutters
the pages of my book,
stirring memory:
a dish of figs, black coffee,
and a brilliant canvas
of cadmium yellow,
black and aquamarine;
below a whitewashed wall
the sea is licking stones.
Here, when I speak,
the sun stands still,
wills me to be complete,
gives me my fill.
Here I am not obsolete:
a word may sing like a knife,
and yet imagination
heals the wounds of life.

*

This morning, cold and clear,
I should be outside
doing something useful,
not writing at all.

Of course, I can't give up:
we're born to strive,
and nothing's better
than to be alive.
What I want then is
for words to burn,
spontaneously combust,
pyrotechnic bursts
turning doubt to dust.

But this morning, clear and cold,
I feel ignorant and old.

*

*

Beauty, wisdom, knowledge
are words engorged like ticks
with ink, too abstract to be
in apposition to my life,
but parasitic nonetheless.

I must give up
my fruitless struggling with words
and throw myself upon the mercies of the world.

Winter will be hard:
frost certainly,
perhaps light snow,
the days shorter,
the ration of heat more meagre.
Tonight a cold wind from the south's
begun to blow.

*

*

The sun has gone and dusk
does strange things to the mind.
There is one star
in the watery pink sky,
an ocean of salmon.
Hospital Hill's become
a brown, beached whale
its hump against the sky
with phosphorescent windows
in its clumsy side.

*

Funeral III

The metaphors the minister employed
were ancient seeds as edible as wheat:
whatever dies becomes the food
of new existence and outlives
death's appetite miraculously.

But the conversation of the pigeons on the roof
broke my willing suspension of disbelief.
Let the dead bury the dead.
I went out and bought hot bread,
took bread and tea
and ate it in the garden.
Eating in the sun
with flies and ants
seemed right.

The Poetry Lesson

Between classes I slide into depression,
take a smoke on the balcony,
listen to the redwing starlings in the trees.
I need someone to hear my confession;
instead I watch my students entering the room.
It's early summer, and the stinkwood in the quad
have grown up to the level of my balcony
which is strewn with broken pigeon nests
and calciferous piles of droppings.

I bring my emptiness inside.
By now my students are domesticated
and call me by my christian name.
Attractive and intelligent, they smile
unenviously at their teacher,
the sixty-four year amiable old fool
with stained teeth, dewlap, and bald head.
I admire their vigour and their skin,
their brilliant teeth, their radiant hair,
the young men's muscles
and the girls' enticing breasts.
I admire their courage that they
at this unnerving time in history
still want to know
the purpose and meaning of poetry.
Biology confers on them such grace and beauty,
and on me a faltering sense of duty.

I give my unchastened children Thomas Hardy:
  'Upon them stirs in lippings mere . . .
  We wonder, ever wonder, why we find us here.'
They have known poetry all their lives,
have written learned essays on it.
'Now tell me what it is,' I ask them.
They are struck dumb, like animals
that smell a yawning emptiness
that waits beyond their years.
Perhaps I have projected onto them
some of my own fears —
that evolution has no purpose,
that mind and spirit, even god,
are only words we use
because we do not understand.
Where can you detect the soul
in our wormlike embryonic state?
Language is a postless gate:
like poems we are gratuitous and ephemeral,
raindrops glistening briefly in the sun.

They look at me expectantly
supposing that my silence
is a pedagogical device:
they don't believe me
when I say it's ignorance.
I will not let them use the words
'transcend' and 'beauty'
because it goes against my sense of duty.

They sense an answer
just beyond their grasp.
Intoxication floods
their solar plexes, bowels and genitals,
and the poem floats free
into the green morning
amazed and filling our silence.
Almost out of range it mingles
with the whistles of the starlings,
and becomes astonishing and strange.

MZI MAHOLA

Next Time Use a Rope

He lived fatherless
For thirty-five years.
Before he was ten
His mother abandoned
For a better life
Of vagrancy and
Hallucinations of meths
Turning her heart into stone
A path he later chose
For escape or success.
In struggles to survive
He lost an eye as well,
The lamp was further dimmed.

One evening they found him groaning
Under a hedge like a bullfrog
Belly-taut with rattex.

I met him coming from hospital
We laughed
About his rodent appetite
He said life was biased.
I said 'Next time use a rope —
You won't fail.'

Two nights later
A school watchman
Found him dangling
Like a maize-cob from a hut roof.
Friends and relatives
Put him deep in a hole.

The Question

People say children are alike
It confounds me
How much they change with time,
When we were young
We didn't ask
Why people threw stones
Into the river
Before they crossed in the evening;
Why we were warned
Never to point a finger
At the sky.
We never asked why elders panicked
When a tree-dassie
Loitered into the yard
Or a hen crowed.
We didn't ask
Why hunters turned home
If a snake or leguaan
Crossed their path,
Why peasants refrained
From ploughing
Or digging holes
Till a dead person was buried.

Now that I'm a parent
Children ask
Why I bury the carcass
Of an animal struck by lightning,
They ask why I worry
When a swarm of bees
Make a hive at my door,
Why I'm troubled
If an owl
Hoots from the roof of my house.

Soon they'll tell me
Why women confront the mother
If the infant refuses her breast
But accepts that of a stranger.

Is it because they are asking
That this world is changing?
Or is the world changing
because they are asking?

There's Nothing Left

I knew that people die out there
Oh brother! Even you?
Your thirty-five years with us
Were short
When in the family we were nine
Now we are stunned.

In prisons and hospitals
We searched for you
All the while
Melancholy waited
Wrapped in white calico
In that mortuary.

We were not there
To soothe your sobs
Hold your soul
When you made that deadly plunge
But God listened.
It don't matter
Who done it
There's nothing left.

CHRIS MANN

Where is the Freedom for Which We Died?

Translated by the poet from his Zulu poem
'Yiyo Lena Inkululeko Esafela Ngayo?'

Whenever I dream during these violent times
I meet up with the martyrs for freedom.

I see Steve Biko again,
and Achmad Timol,
and David Webster,
all, all of them murdered by deeds of hatred.

I also see Nelson Mandela,
a man buried alive in prison
who stepped from his tomb still living
and is the Lazarus of our times.

These are the heroes I think of often,
who knock at the doors of our memory,
who travel around our country
talking together as they look about them
like ancestral spirits of the new South Africa.

Going into the home of a drunkard
they see him beating his wife and children.
'Look at that!' says one of the heroes,
'Is this the freedom for which we died?'

Entering a township
they find the skies full of flames
and people running confusedly round the streets
like termites whose home has been kicked over.
'And look at that!' says another of the heroes,
'Is this the freedom for which we died?'

Going into a school
they see the pupils bickering with the teachers
and two boys stabbing each other.
'And look at that!' says another of the heroes,
'Is this the freedom for which we died?'

Walking the city streets at night
they find the homes locked and barred
as if the people had built their own prisons
and lived inside them huddled in fear.
'I can't believe it!' another of them says,
'Is this the freedom for which we died?'

These are the heroes I think of often,
these are the shades of the new South Africa,
and this is the question they ask the living,
'Where is the freedom for which we died?'

Motos Mota and Fikile Duma

Sickly, sweating, and still woozy at noon,
Motos Mota, a finger short (the mines),
a zip-like scar across one cheek (a fight),
laid off last year (the gold price crashed) has crossed
the goat-bitten, the shanty-crowded hills
to seek direction from a priestess of the shades.

By listless yellow dogs, by washing pegged
like flags in door-sized yards, he grunts his way,
a pilgrim in the limbo-land which rings
the swirling vortex of the sudden town,
where tyres strew the streams, where plastic bags
fly up and flutter in the thorns like captured birds.

Shik-shik, across her flowered linoleum,
MaDuma chants, shaking a beaded switch,
shika-shik, the bangles on her ankles
are strung with pods and bottle-tops, *shik-shik*,
she dances in the spirits for Motos,
the battered, who whops his leathered hands in time.

Swaying, she questions him, and raps the floor
as woe by woe, she draws his heartaches out,
no job, or son, a schoolgirl daughter big with child,
till in a last, rapid stutter of feet,
the gall-bladders of sacrificial goats
bobbing like crinkled brown balloons on her head-dress,

she cries, 'The ancestors, through your neglect,
on you have turned their backs!' Above the shacks
a jet slowly thunders past. 'Lest you remain
a luckless man, a fig without a stem,
by slaughter of a beast, invite them home
and vow, before your kin, to anger them no more.'

'Appease, appease the ancestors again?'
Beside his wrist-watch strap, a year-old strip
of cattle-skin is tied. He stands and sees,
besides a spring, a glossy goat that butts
its mother's wrinkled dugs, and frisks away.
Motos plonks his money down, heads for a shebeen.

A Contemplation of the Soul

1

That green and glittering bird,
hovering in the wild magnolia,
evokes a metaphor for the soul:
a speck of sentient energy
which dips its beak in nectar
and darts through reason's net.

2

Another metaphor's a pearl
where love's potency with soft,
silvery opalescence shines:
its seas are dim eternities
that layer its piece of dust
with the hard radiance of a jewel.

3

The next's hibiscus, a blood-dark,
blood-bright passion to survive
both drought and battering storm:
its one epiphany's a surge
of sap from root to bloom;
labyrinths unfurl from its seed.

4

Another metaphor's a sanctum
where kith and kin, in spirit-shape
debate each day's enigmas:
chin on hand, the private self
presides, a core of being
nurtured in a community of shades.

5

The next's a glass-skinned capsule,
its cockpit luminous with dials,
that journeys through inner space:
the pilot, tuning the telescopes
discovers on the pulsing screens
multiplying images of the self.

6

And last, the soul's a particle
singing in the mind of God,
a metaphor that resonates others,
unless the net is tightened,
the bird languishes in a cage,
a ghost of its darting, glittering days.

To Julia

How beautiful to wake from sleep in your arms
so pale and glimmering in the gloom of night;
no child who stirs in the panic of a dream
could find its fears so tenderly allayed;
no bird which pierces the dark with its cry
could find its solitude so quickly relieved.

I bend to breathe the calm of your body
lithe and mortal in the shroud of sheets;
a nomad who trudges the deserts of despair
could never oasis in such intimate sands;
a buck that lifts its horns from the snow
could never savour such a scent of the spring.

I think of mulberries, dark red in the dusk,
but berries don't bring the warmth of your lips;
I remember a pear, ripening in moonlight,
but fruit cannot yield the fruit of your womb;
I imagine a sun, revolving its planets,
but stars could not gravitate our infants so.

Awake you'd hasten to disclaim these avowals,
holding your image of your self from my words;
but you keep dissolving the void that the mind
keeps blowing between my being and the world,
a linkage which lingers, when dawn intrudes
and breaks shut gates, barbed walls into sight.

Setting the Table

Waking at daybreak, I set the table,
a forum of pine, with place-mat quilts,
red-handled spoons, a bottle of honey,
its label stickied, and bowls like ships,
their holds piled with wheat from far.

Upstairs, a voice entreats the children.
Pouring the milk, I watch as it froths
a momentary lace in a chipped blue jug;
the bread clicks down in the toaster;
it scents the living-room like a hearth.

Entreaties begin to stiffen into ultimata.
Outside the window, in swirls of mist,
a fledgling blur, huffed up in a bush,
stakes out its territory with shrill cries.
The hullabaloo tumults down the stairs.

A tottering son, brandishing a train,
falls headlong on the carpet and bellows;
a tousled-hair daughter, sucking a thumb,
shakes her head at her buttered porridge
and vanishes behind the couch with a cat.

Sleepily the potentates of the family state,
rebuking a squabble, hugging a wanderer,
shaking out tablets, conversing in code,
making and changing a labyrinth of rules,
exert their governance. Silence is called.

A spoon, during grace, digs into a bowl.

Down-Down Lurie

Tom Raath's the red-haired bloke lurching off for a pee.
Craft welder. Makes wrought-iron burglar-bars and
 things.
His leather gloves, his vizored black helmet's on the bar.

Muscleman over there's his cousin. Sells pumps and
 tractors.
His leg's in plaster. Got hammered in a scrum last
 Saturday.
Typical Drikus, head back, glass up, braying with
 laughter.

Chappie Swart's the bald bloke swaying up to the
 dart-board.
Trains horses. The mermaid on his forearm's from navy
 days.
There's a Fender guitar, a red-spangled tux in his
 cupboard.

Boney Riekert chalking up the score's his biggest mate.
Shift-boss at abattoir, breeds Dobermans with the missus.
That's him, wiping his snout, giving the barmaid a stare.

Down-Down belching out the Gent's the owner.
  Widower.
One hell of a chuckling, bustling, cursing bliksem that
  one.
Lonely old gasbag, scooping his belly back into his
  shorts.

Outside the rain's left puddles on the tar of the carpark.
Wetly the hotel's neon glistens its yellows on the
  bonnets.
A cat ghosts by the matt-black bumper of a tow-away
  truck.

Sudden in the silence, a raw burst of laughter from the
  bar.
Shoof! It bursts up like a rocket's showering tail of light.
Then silence again. The dark tall immensity of a rural sky.

———∿∿∿∿ค⊙คผผผ———

JULIA MARTIN

Hospital Night

for my father in a coma at Groote Schuur hospital

It's been only two days
and already I can find my way
in the dark:
unlock the car,
turn the key,
drive up the hill
to the hospital.

The corridors gleam white,
the people let me through, any time.
I know the way to the ICU
I know the smell as you enter the room
I know the way to where
the world's contracted:
this bed where my love lies.

Your face is quiet, softened
by this long sleep
among the machines.
Your body is familiar,
blood of my blood
on the sheets.

But I know nothing
of this big silence,
with only the sound of the ventilator
breathing your broken chest.

I come this way
in the middle of the night
to stand here lost
on the shore
of a white bed
singing the songs you taught me,
singing the tune you sang when I cried,
calling your name
into the low hum
of the hospital's sanitary efficiency.

The specialist says:
'What you're doing is fine.
But we have to inject a note of reality
into all this.'
What does he mean?
Another injection?
A more real world
beyond these walls?

My reality is
I can't see clearly
beyond the simple light
of pain's completeness.
Beyond this bed,

a mist, a dream.
Nothing else is.

I sing to you
from the shore of the bed
but you are far at sea.
And though I know
these songs of home
may never reach you,
this singing is all I can do.

A Small Wind, Breathing

Breathing in, cold sky enters the chest
Breathing out, steam puffs white

Breathing in, the smell of buses in the morning
Breathing out, the late roses are pink and yellow

Breathing in, the roots of the trees grow under the house
Breathing out, each leaf exhales

Breathing in, sun rises over the power station
Breathing out, golden clouds

Breathing in, fear holds the belly
Breathing out, grey seagulls

Breathing in, pain opens in the heart
Breathing out, someone is making breakfast

Breathing in, the touch of hands is warm
Breathing out, a smile

Breathing in, cool space
Breathing out, warm

Breathing in, the skin is porous, receiving light
Breathing out, a small wind moves

PAUL MASON

My Mother's Knowledge

Imaged again, she stirs:
my mother.

She has sloughed out of me blackly, beautifully,
slurring each glaring day into the next,
since her passing.

It is early May. I walk up Cavendish Street,
wearing a jersey although the sun shines.
It is that time of the year that
reminds you of the intimacy of Time,
liquid ambers loosing their leaves,
the sun shedding its last brilliance before winter,
putting me in mind of other times.

Times she guarded the stone of her pain so closely,
forbidding its fall into our common water to ripple ...
    And all the time the brain behind the eyes that
    danced with the multiform meanings of autumn
    was cannibalising itself.

Wintered in, in front of her mirror
She told herself what she had known
from the first diagnosis:
to clothe her remaining days
in the mantle of a deliberate miracle,
its blue penumbra holding us becalmed
until the time.

Knowing the end, she said
'I had hoped it would not be so soon.'

Gone, she has gone:
my mother.

ZAKES MDA

'Mamane'

Mamane
These walls are echoing your name
And the gardens grow such beautiful flowers
Look Mamane the flowers
We never used to write about flowers
We sang only about bazookas
The music of the guns
The smell of sulphur
Fires burning
Bulldozers like tanks of war
Petrol bombs
Ours were songs of war
They say things are changing
But for us they remain the same
Life has not been kind Mamane
Houses are rubble
Burning human flesh smells stronger
It overwhelms delicate garden scents
We build Mamane
We so much want to build
The sounds of the guns are so loud
We can't hear the birds sing
Only the guns
Our loves never died still

That is why we continue to have the strength
To fight and die
Until we can smell the flowers
And we can hear the birds
But these walls reverberate so strongly
With your name

Dove

Peripheral, exhausted, washed out
onto the shore of dreams
like a ribbon of sea-weed
the figure lies splayed.

This is no golden coast
no beach of bronze langour
of sun-seeped sand.
This is the tawdry sub-tropical
strip at the edge of the tepid sea.

I think I shall turn to religion:
not Christ — I am tired
of failed saviours —
only the cool incense breath of the holy spirit,
the dark anonymity of the nave,
yes, the comforting womb of the church;
I think I shall
fall there prostrate, wings splayed,
hard red breasts pressed against the pew,
on a Monday morning
(when the baby's asleep,
his sister at playschool),

the woman sweeping the church
thinking I am struck down with devotion,
or, seeing, sideways,
the flight of worn-out spirit of woman;
then maybe the church words will soothe
my barbed feathers;
cool pebbles washed by the sea;
no; I doubt it;
I think I shall have to make my own prayer
for the quotidian demands of hard day — swill it round
like pills with black coffee —
no; make it, rather,
mouths full of muffins at my mother's breakfast
breaking the night;
night of spectres of dead aspirations and
the baby crying and
crying, coo to me caressing voice
give me warm milk and
deep sleep again
deep sleep;
there in the cool of the church
I shall chew my rough words,
my coarse-grained words,
spirits of women give me patience
and love to unblock the ducts
of love for my children, conduits
of love for the father
of my children;
inject me with potency
to wipe away this anaesthetic veil
keeps me from entering life lightly again;

give me strength to remember my love,
give me love —
no; I shall not pray for transfiguration,
for centuries long, long ago longing for peace
of Madonna and Child;
less, less, give me less, only
strength for the tasks
of love.

Ruth Miller

You were an ordinary woman,
I imagine,
crabby even.
(Who would not be
with the petit-bourgeois trappings —
vibracrete fencing your box-house in Yeoville,
I imagine,
and tidy lawn, drawing the lines —
keeping the crumbling facade
of your marriage clean?)

So deep you hid your baying heart,
tight you kennelled it nightly,
slipping fragments of desire
when the words came knocking on the archetraves
of bone around the hard closed door,
prizing through to the nervous flesh,
the quivering, raw, red flesh
let us out
(though your fingers fretted to the bone to keep them in);

such depth of sorrow you kept
encased, scarab-like,
unadmitted, unadmitted,
that readers, knocking on the hard case of metaphor,
    plead
let us in let us in.

God who gave ordinary women
such grief such weight of pain
that Sisyphus wise they must bear it
up hill each day!

I, being less exceptional,
an ordinary woman too, more blessed
hearing my second baby's babbling in the room below
am quite sure, now,
working again through the shroud of your words,
the death of children is as you show —
irredressible, absolute —
no elegy could ease its pain.

No wonder
the stone grew hard inside your arachnid heart
eating you inside out.

Poem for my Mother

Like Anne Sexton's daughter, long ago
I called on God
                    knows what, something some-
one else instead of you:
                                        finally
having fallen from the horse that dragged
me, head hit by hooves like coconuts
clapping with every galloping pace,
finally
            having gathered up your
daughter like a fallen pod,
                                    having
watched her dragged by the demented horse,
finally
            held to your heaving breast,
sensing your staggering shock
                                        I asked
if I wasn't too heavy for you;

only seven, holding the secret
of separation so tight,
it seems, seamed to my breast, over seasons of
years, that even now the unclean the
ambiguous severing of selves,
mother and daughter, sears through my love.

Sunday Night — On My Own — After the Uitenhage Shootings

There is not much doubt, tonight,
                              if I could paint I would not
be writing, but painting the
                    night air, the sweet wind, tonight.

At first I longed to paint trees,
                    like gums, or maritime pines,
on open squares like on the
                    flats — Italian ochre and
palpable thick-veined olive;
                    but it is the air, through the
green, across the flats, blowing
                    the balm of thick night air that
makes me want the soft stroke on
                              canvas, thick layers of air,
smelling of lemon, blown through
                    pine needles, blown through pepper
trees in the square here in this
                    Observatory, blowing
the mobile gentle birds at
                    my barred window, ignoring
me, not minding, I can go
                    on writing wanting to paint
the wind so soft, tender as
                    a contented mother or
confident lover, him-self,
                    wholely, tolerating this

my wanting to blow away,
                    to still, the week's anxious fear;
it stirs despite the people
              killed this week, despite carnage,
breathes despite the dead, despite
                          murder, inability
of the weak to keep death fixed
                        in front of body, being
mind, despite desire for god
                of gentle wind, balm of night;

by the day's light tomorrow
they will have stopped the mourning;

and the wind will rip again
exposing
          no time
                  for balm.

For Adrienne Rich

In the quiet of the house on my own
with your poems that dusk slowly taking
me your poems tender making love your
words bit by reaching bit caressed me touched
me gently your words addressed to me then.

Loving palpably black on white I love
the feel of your words. The common language
I could not have known I was dreaming of
gently you speak in language lovers use;

and as with love force me to face the lack
admitting longing to use this language
lovers use too to speak too to reach out

leaving gaping loss like love always leaves.

KOBUS MOOLMAN

Autumn

Now the street of my childhood is again
ablaze with the rust of last year's leaves.
Again the ground crackles and shuffles
beneath my feet, disintegrating into flakes
of forgetfulness, the shards of a nostalgia
sweet and sharp. I am cut each year
by the trees on this old street — the street
of my childhood — buried now beneath the dreams
of my bones, a heart brittle with regret,
unable to find that perfect pensiveness
cradled like a brand in the arms of the trees.

Untitled

If I were a boat dear love
I could cradle you over
the dark and heaving waves
though wind and lightning chased
fears into your sleep
and deep currents wound ropes
of rapaciousness around your wings.

If I were a road my love
I could roll direction relaxed through
the tangle of time's fierce involvement
Distance would conceal you
from fate's cruel comedy
where lust and greed range
rewarded with long life and prosperity.

But I am only human love
and born without such miracles of imagination
I am dry glass and shattered dust
I am mute seed ignorant of
what blossom I may be or weed —
A sadness only silence can utter
is all the bread I have to break for thee.

SEITLHAMO MOTSAPI

the man

an almost forgotten acquaintance
was in town recently
i noticed that it started raining
just as he ambled in

i remember him as a simple man
growing up, we all wanted
to be doctors, lawyers & teachers
so the blood could ebb out of the village

my friend had much more sober dreams
he asked the heavens to grant him
the imposing peace of the blue-gum in his backyard
and that all the poor send him their tears
so he could be humble like the sun
so the red wax of the stars would not drip onto him

i remembered that man today
and all i think of is his unassuming radiance
like that of a blushing angel

as for his dreams
he tells us
whole forests invade his sleep at night
so that there's only standing room
for the dreams

tenda

i look at you
& you remind me of all the mountains
i haven't seen or embraced
& since you are like every one of us
you rise out of my heart
with the craggy serenity of kilimanjaro
enduring like prophecies
peaceful like distances
since you are like all of us
eternal like every river
even when the sea claims us
for me you carry affirmations
a sprout in the parch, a mend in the rend
water from an ancient well
& since every one of us
carries the seeds of a storm within him
since the mountains come to rest
in the breast of every one of us
beginning the long journey across the desert
since the forests & the skies & the faces of children
overflow with the lessons of love
for all to learn
i will always remember you
& your face that is the end of all roads
poetry will never travel
i will remember you
when i have learned the rustle of rivers
when i have learnt the inconvenient gestures of
    compassion
when i have learned to be infinitely present
& yet invisible like the sky

dear mother

mother i lie awake at night
& soon you have every grain of my soul to yourself
& soon every one of my thoughts is a remembrance
of past bruises & resilient wounds
i listen to songs that are full of holes
& the melodies are waistless like dust
so i spit at them
since you throb like a storm in my heart
the past now appears as a knot of furies
with blades running into my flesh
the past now appears as a despicable wave
of ebbing profanities

mother i lie awake at night
weary like every penitent
& naked like an infidel
my wounds distort the landscape of embraces
my gait straggles like a lament
at those who look after the hills
& i cry mother
because fire burns those who play with it
& those who dig holes only fall into them

i come to you at night mother
the mountains, the songs, the herds, the children
& the sea that takes over the hills each night
& the sands that run out or the sky at sunset
& the familiar faces that sprout from the rocks
i rest them all in my heart mother
so the perfume of your love can bless them

so i lay me down each night
at the edge of the ancient forest
while i await the mesej
from those who work our clay in their infinite patience
that is older than the skies
i lay me down each night
where the road flowers into a garden
& where boulders start to sing
like breezes or children
so those who have piled darknesses into their hearts
can find salvation again

& so i cry to you mother
soon it will be the time of harvests
soon those who preach love & handshakes
will ascend the altars & the skies
so the poor can make their peace with tomorrow
so the lacerations will return to their screams
those of us who still break the ritual bread
will rise with their steel & their holy noises
so the bruises can bend their knee
to our hasty thuds

& so i cry to you mother
i am your son who has returned
i cry to you mother
i am your son who needs cleansing
so i can become a sun again
so i become a boulder again
where the earth can rest her simple redemptions

mantsi

i've learnt love
from absences
that is, i've been like the stars
solemn & wistful

but tomorrow
all the stars will plummet
to their inevitable ash

already
i see the songs have begun
to resemble you

so, sister of the perennial dawn
we are coming for you
me & my shrunken heart & my doleful skies

SALLY-ANN MURRAY

Shifting

Within the drifting, whale-wide wallows of
Your body, deep in sleep, my head hears
The windy rainbeat gusting under
And on and into the shape of history.

We sleep — you sleep — while workers wake
    themselves
Down at the docks, up near the Union Flour Mills:
The cold, metallic shove of shunting hits
Its hulking, thudding bulk into the future.

Your sleeping shape does not resist my touch.
Nor does it form an answer tangible.
Outside of time you wheeze, a staggered snore,
Unpunctured by the whistle of the shift.

ANDRIES WALTER OLIPHANT

The Hunger Striker

I hear my voice like the sombre rattle
of a diviner's bones:
After a life of eating porridge
with my hands from a dixie
I dream of waking up at home.

I sit at a table with a knife and fork.
The earth's edible crust
steaming in my porcelain plate.
I drink the sky distilled from a glass.
There is happiness the size of freedom in my cup.

But then I hear the stout voices of men in shorts
washing tin plates up.
The house in which I left a wife and child
is now deserted
and infested with rats and mice.

I go into the street and come across myself
shackled in leg irons
digging a hole in the sidewalk
big enough to hold my shrinking body.
The spade I was given has become an axe.

The baker from my childhood is in his doorway
with flour on his hands.
He speaks and I see
roasted corn spill from his mouth
like a praise poem to labour and productivity.

A girl passes on a bike and waves at me.
It looks like my daughter
in the clothes of my wife.
I cannot free my hands from the axe to wave back.
I try to raise my leg but the irons restrain me.

My neighbour passes in an empty bus.
Through a broken window
he shouts at me:
The earth is full of yellow bones
which you must dig up!

I laugh like one immersed in life's conviviality
amid table cloths and serviettes.
Amid the repertoire of knives and forks,
the bright taste of pain
strikes me like a sharpened axe.

After Life

in memory of my father

In the month of your star
the sky teems
with barbels, carp, yellowtail and snoek.
On the banks of the Blesbok
you cast a line.
I cast a line at Dwesa from the rocks.
I see the split cane and the conoflex bend.

Late afternoon my car drones
through the rain.
I drive through the city
with the image of your catch
and our laughter
to the fire in your bed.

The gown they dressed you in
mimics the colours
of my infancy: yellow, blue and red
rectangles on a birthday shirt.
Your hands with which you speak
refer to udders round with milk.

And the truck you drove laden with pumpkins,
tomatoes, carrots, beetroot
and the fruit that kept me out
of other people's orchards.
When your land was taken
your right to live was confiscated.

How far did you cycle through that night?
With brown bread and pilchards
you kept us all alive.
While I made wire cars
with fish tails
which nobody would buy.

I came with a booth full of memories
swimming through my head like fish.
The rain was at the window
beating out a message which I could not read.
You said it was your mother, the midwife
and left me with your taciturn hat and pipe.

Blue

There's blueness in the bush.
It rises from your chest,
your sweater and your vest.

It bursts from your pants
and from the sand
between your sunned legs.

I see the blueness
of the light
that plays about your mouth.

My love,
I drink the sky
from your perfect head.

KAREN PRESS

Needlework

From my needle small birds fly:
pink lattice feathers, leafgreen eyes,
yellow crests, plum spikes for tails.

Beside me on the metal pole
tubing threads down from a plastic bag
as thick and soft as a pound of liver:

your blood, midnight red stitches
of the deep needle filling you;
mine chainstitching bright birds.

Dispossessed Words

found poem
for Jessie Tamboer, who set herself alight and burned to death
because she could no longer provide food for her children

Trucks carried 40 000 blacks to the southern edge of the
     desert.
I cannot say anything about my future now.
          We had a very beautiful view
          and this was the first time I saw my father cry.

They said 'Old man, are you moving?'
I took a crowbar, pulled the house down.
I cannot say anything about my future now.

                              *

   A man must have a dumping ground.
   Every rabbit has got a warren.
   A native must have a warren too.

                              *

Sometimes I cry, I
the absolute poor
I am sick to death of watching my ruin.

                              *

We had a very beautiful view of the sea —
                    This was refused.

                              *

Uncovering rubbish bins, I ask, could it not be that
    something has been thrown in here —
just a little something that I can chew?

This was refused.

*

At times she would just suddenly start sobbing without
    any apparent reason.

The absence of love.
There is no way you can describe that hunger.
Shining clean pots and jars:
There was no food whatsoever in the house.

*

She was immediately engulfed by flames but did not utter
    a sound as she walked around the yard burning.

The ashes of one household are collected by another for
    the bits of coal.
If you want to survive you must make a plan.

I cannot say anything about my future now.

ARJA SALAFRANCA

12.53pm

It's Sunday.
Flies buzz in and out the house.
Today the world stops turning.
The odd car chases its fumes,
the birds chorus a solid cliché.

Hot water trickles onto the grass
from a hosepipe lying in the sun.
People turn a crisp brown
despite the high protection gels and creams.
They fall asleep, and wake up
glaring red on one side,
splotched with dirt on the other.

They clean up the swimming pool
retrieving the soggy paper cups
thrown in after last night's party,
rake the garden of cigarette butts.
Bottles of wine and beer clang in a
big black rubbish box.
Then they'll sleep away the afternoon
waking to wash away the hangover with Eno.

Slap the flat tubes of boerewors
and slabs of steak
onto the hissing grill.
Watching the aroma rise and drift
next-door, laughing loudly into the
sunshine, drinking to the celebration of
Sunday with ice-cold cans.

The motorbike screeches across Norwood
looking for Algernon Road. Someone buys
insect repellent. Someone buys rolls.
Someone tosses away the crumpled remains
of a newspaper. Someone smooths the white sheets
and lays the duvet carefully on the bed.

BARBARA SCHREINER

Chain Reaction

I
Living there   but not a resident
while out walking
uncoiling the taut springs of his back
warped from weeding   and watering
his jaw met a white fist.
His daydreams stumbled
knocked against white-painted walls
dog-high gates
the rhythm of kaffir-klapping rage
until there was too much blood
and his mind sprawled
lurching to the hot reality
of tar   and boots
swinging to meet ribs

He lay in the road like garbage
scattered by remorseless dogs
and his thoughts shivered like a mirage
in the desert of suburban gardens.

II
In the cold whip of winter
midday and mad
he burned his wife
turned her   among plastic plates
and sunlight soap
from dusky black   to pale
peeling like paint from an old door.
Her child cries for the breast
pink now like raw pork
and dreams of flames.
I rage with the pain
and phone an ambulance
and wait   with her
and the smell of charred flesh and paraffin
and the statement she might have made
melted like plastic onto her lips

I sing to her child
dark   like the skin she once wore
dark   like the tunnels of a father's soul
dark   like anger   like night
like sleep   and hot chocolate
soft like hope   and milk
I sing without words
sound without sense
against the cold wail of human winter.

Hadedah

The flower-bed predator sinks its picked beak like a
    piston,
spreads its legs like a suburban cowboy, places its weight
and levers out of the ground. The big bird is related to
    the ibis

and is exotic. It takes its place among things that we
    know,
though they came without being named or naming,
without references, the visible inhabitants in their own
    space

with ours in common. The most we have said
is that they were omens and make a very loud, uncivilized
    noise,
but they climb with imagination — above my house

they bank in flights and top the lopped horizon,
slice fat clouds and dip away into the trough,
cut through jacaranda and succulence smells,

wood fire and anthracite smells and swipe the light
from the East Rand gold towns. Mine heads wink
like nuggets in dumps and streams, like steel fly eyes,

wheels of fortune, *the* wheel, and they climb, over people
   singing
home in trains and other people talking softly
saying *Next year in Jerusalem, London, Sydney,*

over neon paradises, shebeen kingdoms
and corrugated churches on earth. They level out,
leave behind the thatch and bougainvillaea,

slasto, rosaries, private Edens that were not always good,
but always there, over dunes, rivers, mountains,
lakes, jungles, ancestral homes, the unmarked graves

of sleeping cultures, until, when no one can see,
they catch a warm thermal to ride on and upwards
and out of the world.

Westpark

for PRS and GF

It says *Van Zyl Straat* on the green street-sign
near where sons come to bury their mothers very far
away from the Old Country. Westpark is where we come

to put years back in the ground, lay new reefs
and strata and make them precious. It is too dry
for lawns. Burying in the veld is conceptual

and the highest thing is the communication tower on the
    koppie.
If the dead pick up sound waves there is no peace
but they hear news and relatives saying

A man walks into a delicatessen and says waiter ... Yes,
and she was telling me this only last week.
Sons come to bury their mothers. People come to bury
    their own.

Making patterns on the plain pine with clods and grit,
and then only shapes, we fill the hole ourselves
with spades, not handed on, but spliced back

into the mounds either side and taken up again. We lay
    new reefs,
put away a generation, and being alive, cry,
bless, praise, glorify, extol, honour, magnify and laud,

then afterwards learn to look away, and drive away, and
    later
do the shopping — the lost having been gathered up,
    and patted down
in the language that the world was made in.

———ᴧᴧᴧᴧᴚᴚ◎ᴚᴚᴧᴧᴧ———

DOUGLAS REID SKINNER

Arrival

Vitaque mancipio, nulli datur, omnibus usu.
Lucretius

Throughout the long day following
A near-but-never-quite-asleep night
Propped across two armchairs in
The ward where she lay lost to the world
(Crying out three times in dream-filled sleep),
I sat at your mother's bedside reading
Wilfred Owen, which ends with his death
On a bank of the Oise mere days from the end
Of the First World War's mad slaughtering ...

While she worked so hard to bring you forth,
The boy she'd harboured for three whole seasons
Of a year marked by unceasing change,
The tides of pain growing steadily worse
Until the relief of chemicals eased
Her tension and brought to an end your stay
In the water-cushioned bliss of her body ...
Yours, shocked by the cool air, covered
From head to toe with blood and vernix,

Your dark eyes staring from a mis-shapen,
Alien and here-to-witness head wrapped
In the cradle of her exhausted arms
And suckling for the very first time.
Unhinged, I couldn't stop myself shouting,
'My baby! My baby! It's my baby.'
In that brief moment, you belonged to us
In a way that will never be true again.
You were wholly ours and only ours —

In a way that will never be true again.

264 THE HEART IN EXILE

Utamaro, Observed

Across a passage   of damp wallpaint
steadily peeling   away from the wall
silver braids   of water fall
into a bath   of steam that rises
past the angles   of half-closed door
while the view   that goes
from room to room   to where absorbed
in what she's doing   leaning above
her faint reflection   carefully testing
the temperature   — too hot, too cold? —
is not of someone   recognised
when all that can   be seen in light
and shadow is   a pair of legs
muscle and skin   tightly stretched
by a body bent   almost double
a torso curving   down from where
rounded cheeks   (and narrow line
of shadow where   they softly meet)
curve in until   they disappear
two halves of fruit   tucked neatly into one another   giving with
slightly increased   indrawn breath
a sudden glimpse   of darkly fragrant
curling hairs   (memory! memory?)
recollected   Rome and Greece
ancient Indian   bas-reliefs
shadowed bedrooms   everywhere
the brushstrokes of   a master painter

capturing neither   face nor line
of throat and shoulder   the room in which
they sat and talked   but rather this
the hidden heart   whose giving's all
we know of where   we come from and
where, perhaps   we end

Now, Years Later

Is it wistfulness or anguish brings
at five a.m. or seven in the evening
heartfelt lament that always begins
'Remember how we used to ... then ...'
trailing off and never quite ending?

Last night it came to you again,
staring through the car's side window
at streets that flowed past in a blur
of neon glare, houses and trees,
and behind them all, the resolute

dark, steep ridges of the mountain
gliding wholly unperturbed
on and on through darkness ...
when you launched into mid-stream,
beginning with 'Remember when ...'

rowing round in widening circles,
cataloguing additional, new
shades of regret pulled out from
the deep and almost infinite drawer
of emotional explanations for

feeling the way we sometimes do —
filled with fear, abandoned,
nothing but darkness up ahead,
everything good already gone,
experienced '... when we were ...'

responsible for so much less ...
your voice, as always, trailing off
into the silent houses and trees,
cars and people flashing past,
the dark, steep ridges of the mountain

gliding wholly undisturbed
across the wheeling cast of stars,
an enormous, full moon rising
over the bay to light the hidden
municipalities of the heart.

Love brings its own defeats with it,
its price is nothing less than all
those brilliant, blissful years
replaced by knowing, gradually,
more what was, less what will be.

KELWYN SOLE

Lost City

Imaginary beings, in a real landscape
Kim Stanley Robinson

By the Kong Gates we paused
but could not think
                  beyond the new vistas
given to us unfolded. Two alabaster parrots
betrayed our trust
                  and did not move. We meandered
through baobabs, rain forest, a desert
past exotic llamas — a world in one country —
interrupting no creature of breath. Latex rocks groaned
beneath our hard heels, and an electric cable
        whipped the breeze
hissed.
                  At the Valley of Courage
there was only the splat and slurry of piped water
awaiting us playmates
                and our fall.

All our cities are lost. By the one
armed bandits we slouch down and forget
to weep.

The Beaching of the 'Mendi'

1
In amongst the dogs
dropping turds on the beach
rich food of their white owners

and little children
holding on each other's hands
little crabs of brown and pink
with growing carapaces

in the new reformed South Africa

while their parents smile
at each other, frostily

or look the other way

and young men with balls
and insistent bats and muscles
ogle
      young women
turning near-naked torsos
spitted on the sun

suddenly all notice

a shape indistinct
among the waves

at first can't see

so pick up hot
sunglasses lazily

then jump up
scream, slip, and run
in panic run

2
on a newly deserted beach
bobbing from the waves

a hand claws
slowly up the sand
spidering its fingers

a flesh-flayed foot drags
leg and hip
ribs a marimba for the wind

ears separate
grotesque sea shells

the bones complain
shudder and rattle
at last home free

talking fragments
multiply to multiply
strive to rebuild their life
upon the shore

a head with absent eyes
rolls and rolls and rolls
inside the wind

wonders how it will come to rest

The *Mendi*, a troopship carrying black soldiers of the South African Native Labour Contingent to the war in France, was sunk in the English Channel in February 1917 with the loss of over 600 men. Ever since, 'Mendi Day' has been remembered (and often commemorated by African nationalists) as a symbol of black courage, national sentiment and sacrifice in the face of white racism and indifference.

The Face and the Flag

1
The baby, in his crib, dances with his fists
beating the air, purring 'aaa' or humming 'mmm'.
A flat note.
The mother is ironing linens on a rough wooden table.
We can hear the insistent thud of dull iron on cloth.
She is chatting quietly with her teenage daughter.
The two voices are alike; the one could be
an echo of the other.
Their voices merge, run with our whispering.

'You're right,' says Sticks.
'The real revolution starts when millions of people
begin to move, feeling as one it is
no longer possible to turn back, that
all their bridges have been burnt
behind them.'

Henry and Bongi are smoking. James
plucks cursorily at his guitar
slotting chords into the night

which rattle down to earth and are lost,
amber disks, in the machines of poverty.

'Our job is to give it a good shove
and get the whole thing going ... like ...
a stone ... you know? an avalanche?'

Other voices outside the house.
A banging door. A barking dog.
The dark, kink-haired mother, annoyed
by our vain theorising, goes outside
to lean over the railing, and look
at the beautiful night sky — the horizon
of her sight — without seeing it.
Her thin voice, her tired eyes blotched
by some timeless reproach, her skin ravaged
by skin-lightening cream and work
are familiar to us. She is at that age
when well-dressed women are still desirable,
and the others are all finished up.

She is thinking:
'As if they wouldn't do better
to try and earn a little money.' A while ago
she said 'It's okay. We land on our feet
every time, God knows, like a cat that some kid
throws out of the window at regular intervals.
It's already something to be able to feed
our faces every day.'

    Her husband
had wanted to be a painter; he's a sign
painter. HENRY'S INSTANT SIGNS.

They haven't loved each other for a long time.

2
Tonight the wind is a child
teasing the eucalyptus brooding
over the tiny park nearby,
a foreign body chiding the lips
of our national moon.

The songs of resistance
are more muted now
                    trade unions
praise their politicians, expectant
of a better world.

                    Limousines
filled with executives
still grease the multiracial
freeways. Books forgotten
with their covers red
are now an item up for sale.

There is a quiescence which longs
to break itself.

3
Now that the streets are full of our flags and us
          whose tongue
spans the distance from shop window to shop window
          as we march
onwards to the rally's end (teargas weeping its
          own demise)
and the work of placing brick upon brick to build
          we can guess

will soon begin and our imaginations desires yearn
        to the future
a new history for us in which to grow forgetful of
        the crowd
begun to move apart each head above its own lately
        created hope
beneath your glad your apprehensive face your banal
        flesh asserts
a familiar world of flat feet of allergies of
        eyes itching
and tiredness the dubious blessing of over-earnest
        comrades
surreptitiously from your sight's corner you watch
        one person
her hair a black cloud you imagine perfume kindness
        despite her
che guevara t-shirt then to be noticed you shout out
        viva viva
but begin to dream of a space to make love again
        to know
the joyful smell of sex again, your body freshly
        trembling
and start to drag all your noble thoughts behind you
        a puppy
protesting as it stirs back to old memories, old
        needs
wish the romance of the nation done wish for tangible
        loving.

4
And five years from now?

As you are fat and pleased
with what the interim
has gained
        and your
own heroic past stares
in ill-concealed boredom
from the expressions
of your wife and friends
as you reminisce
at countless dinner parties

(her che guevara t-shirts
with his image buried
beneath dashikis,
pin-striped shirts)

what if one night you hear
softly at first, then
louder, ever more insistent,
the roar of throats
back in the street?

as you look over
your balcony with the lattice
digging into your nipples
so you stretch further,
do you see that face
in the crowd below you?

you, who want to lean forever
on the comfort of your victories
your defeats:

(exulted, angry, much
like one you used to know)

that still distant night
the moon smirks down

and what you once had fought for
begins to slide from what
you now perceive; slides
into the frown on your own brow
puzzled at its new surrender

as everyone except you marches anew
in a democracy of shapes and colours
for socialism

(you have so much to lose)

comrade, traitor, lover, friend —
will you dismount into the street?

Part 1 of 'The Face and the Flag' is adapted from Victor Serge, *Birth of Our Power* (Writers & Readers Publishing Co-operative, London, 1977).

WILMA STOCKENSTRÖM

Africa Love

Like Inhaca facing the coast, I'm turned
to you, with my soft mouth, my breasts.
Like her I nestle in a bay of kindness,
I grow, coral-like but without fail
closer to you, my mainland. What
does the mercantile marine back
on the battering seas mean to me?
Cunningly my dripping mangroves advance
in tepid waters step by little step.
How long before I merge with your wide
cashew-nut forests, before we fit into each other,
your reed-overgrown arm around me,
your brown body my body.

Translated by Johann de Lange

MARK SWIFT

Home Thoughts

There is no road home
    for home is where the heart is.
        We are
        voyagers, we carry
our journeys within us. Privateers,
    we run before a fickle wind.
    Each day defines a course; its fixed
        imperative. Out on the jet
streams, adrift for days, we navigate
    the tide-bound globe. We are all
    Columbus, quaffing
sour water under creaking stars
        till moonfall.

    I fly, as unerring
as a bird, between two departures.
        One lies
dark, skeletal; the other is verdant,
    a wildness of birds and gunfire.
        With renegades
    from every corner of the shrinking
world, I discuss, duty-free,
        the love of distant friends,
    the lure of the sun

and the arid wines of another place. We share
        the east, the south; go west
    before closing time.
Far above, on migratory trails,
        the gypsies at heart
        fly home and away.

Windvogel Mountain

(Cathcart, Eastern Cape)

From this fastness, this haphazard
    castle of stone and air, we straddle
        the galleries daubed by San.
Below us, on painted rock, the long-dreamed,
    long-dead kudu are brought to their knees
        by pin-pricks.

Hills away, a slow-coach train draws
    a thin, black line
        across ochre impasto. The centipede
of iron and its distant halt, a half-baked
    town on the rim of the world, betray
        the advance of history, of hair-trigger men
        on the make.

This is the landscape of the brutal mind,
    beyond the reach of compass
        or intention. It is cradle
and deathbed, slung between poles of dawn
    and darkness, of fire and ice.

Below us, in their warrens, the hunters cowered
    as quarry, driven to earth by shod
        and blinkered centaurs. Men of the sky,
at home on the wind, they were brought to their knees
        with their painted prey.

Waterlines

for Jack Cope, Richard Rive, Steve Bell and Roy Webber

Life exacts a death
for every year
        on the water's edge. The damp sun
    leaves clean slates
            where their heads
            and gestures
were daubed on our walls.

We home in on the river
to hear its garbled vernacular;
        its phrases of mumbled regret.
    Each year it springs to life, trips
            on its tongue, pronounces
        a death. On the path
where the water slurs its vowels
    we leave the bones of our shadows,
resurrect; toil on again
        to the source.

All existence flows to that end, it runs
uphill. We pouch our mouths
        at air and words as we salmon
    down to plunge upstream
            through time. Men
    and rivers die; they are eaten
by earth. On the gnawed banks
        a child fumbles at a sextant
    of hands; his small
            paper ship goes out.

In the shallows of our rooms
we fish for words, cast about
        to express our grief. Down the road
    the water garbles
            its sermons; the river unfolds
        its winding-sheet
over small paper ships
            and men.

Down to the Wire

At Charlie's. For Oona

We burned in the slow
      heat of a summer
      turned sunny side up
but sombre with misgivings.
      Stilting girl, as strange
      as fact, you made fiction
of my fears; lies of
   the comforting truths.

On the billows of your bed
      we made
      love like a tide, tossed
      high and dry on a dune
      of sheets
when the last wave broke.
         No-one drowned; we dreamed instead.
      We clutched at straws and
      survived each other.

No tides batter here, there is
      only the flat, watery waste
      of damp fen wrested
         from the inland sea.
         Horizons shrank
in the undersea, upstairs room. We explored
      the known indefinite; found ciphers
         to unspoken codes.

There was you. There was me. The
   telephone played its numbers
      game; totting up short-
   circuits of loud and static
      anger. We went down to the
   wire, subtracted but not
      diminished. I still rise as a
   Lazarus, up from our sheets, those
shrouds of fear and
         silence. Together, we kill to resurrect;
         day after winter's day.

Shadows on the Wall

Under the toiling tree-tops, always
   in a high wind, my aunt's house
      sagged under dripping
  eaves. Window-warped,
     barred to the light, it kept
       her darker secrets. Beneath
the hunchbacked sofa, behind the laden
  sideboard, the past was put
     to rights; never swept away.

Outside, a living, sprung and tender
  world lay breathing and open.
     On green mornings, berry-mad,
  we scratched like chickens
     in the undergrowth. Hot on the
      warpath, armed to the teeth,
we stalked our childhoods till bedtime.

Adrift on feathers, creaking through
  the long nights, I followed the moon
     as it tugged at its tides
  for no reason or rhyme. In her
     sanctum, her spinstered room
      with its china and lace,
a lover gloomed down out of tarnish.
  Her dresses, wallflowers
     in a wardrobe, had ceased their dance.

Alone in her brown study, she pinched
   her pennies, counted her griefs
      as blessings coined
by a thriftless God. The telephone
   slept on its cradle, no visitors
      called, and death when it came
   did not knock.

Augury

Once more, one last time
around the water. Evening
is coming in. The jacaranda
blossoms are raining
on the path, exploding
quietly underfoot.

We will leave silently, driving slowly
through the gathering dark.
We have all we need: wild flowers
are as close as we can hope
for of heaven. Our time
is short. Our hands
are full. We know
we are at war.

Still Feeling

Things change, shift
immeasurably, immensely.
Remain the same

That after all is the all
of it: setting out early
to find the way back
to where we are

*

The body is far wiser
than the brain, it makes
its home where it finds itself
thinks less of exile

It is a shell held
to the sea that speaks
its own endlessness

*

Turn loss to a hard small
stone in the palm of your hand
clasp it till it breaks

your skin

Early

Things
        come and go
Then
        let them.
Robert Creeley: 'A Step'

I wake into the fishscaled
myriad mirrored glint
of myself, the miraculous
flow and counterflow, unfathomable
surge and retreat.
Implosive, this morning
happenstance is a silent dance
of becoming and having-
been and dreaming. Everything
bears down on this single
moment, this single space.
There are so many words
that cannot touch the heart
of this secret self-invention.

This then: this day just begun —
I am a point of gathering, agglomeration
of body-stuff, mind-stuff, song
and sight, emotion and the faint sleep-
scent of skin, touch and skin's soft
giving. This then: this day just begun
moves endlessly through everything
I am become. This then:

there is everything that we call me and you:
surge and retreat, the illimitable
roar of this morning's heaped silences.

MATTHEW VAN DER WANT

The Ville Blues

I wish I had a car
I'd drive out to Rosebank
I'd do lunch with my Filofax
I'd catch a serious film
Like Sireno da Bergarek
I might never come back
To Rosettenville

But if I hear another Ha de da
        if I hear another little dog bark
        if I hear another v 6 car
I think I'm gonna crack
In Rosettenville

I wish I had some cash
I'd buy a new electric guitar
With an amp that sounds real hectic, Ah
I'd write some real deep songs
Something esoteric
Eat my dust
Eric ... Clapton
In Rosettenville

But if I hear another pinball machine
     if I hear another schoolgirl scream
     if I hear another cafe owner's dream
I think I'm gonna crack
In Rosettenville

I wish I had some shades
I'd look cool on the bus
The southern girls would ache with lust
But I'd just sit there & look mysterious
Like I had the world sussed
Like I hadn't noticed the rust
In Rosettenville

CHRIS VAN WYK

Memory

Derek is dangling on the kitchen chair
while I'm shuffling about in a flutter of flour.
Mummy is making vetkoek on the primus.
Derek is too small to peer over the table,
that's why Mummy has perched him on the chair.
His dummy twitters so he's a bird.

I'm not that small; I was four in July.
I'm tall enough to see what's going on;
I'm a giraffe and the blotches of shadow
on the ceiling and the walls
from the flames of the primus and candle
are the patches on my back.

Daddy's coming home soon
from the factory where they're turning him into
a cupboard that creaks,
but the vetkoek are sizzling and growing
like bloated gold coins,
we're rich!

This is the first vivid memory of childhood.
Why have I never written it all down before?
Maybe because the pan falls with a clatter
and the oil swims towards the twittering bird.
Mummy flattens her forearm on the table
stopping the seething flood.

As she does so she pleads with the bird to fly away,
but quietly so as not to ruffle his feathers.
But my brother clambers off the chair
as if he has all the time in the world.
Sensing danger, the twittering gives way to a wail
and the giraffe's patches flare on the restive walls.

Ma gives a savage scream that echoes across the decades
and cauterizes my childhood like a long scar.

PETER WILHELM

On Her Departure

I have not been faithful to you,
he said as she flew away:
but when I think about the afterlife,
or afterword, something ahead
beyond
the catcalls of foreign acclaim,
whatever it is you're looking for,
or my own ponderous bitterness
and its fate:
then I consider, in any case,
neither were you to me.

So what's that, in the eye of eternity?
Love isn't a hacksaw
to hack up the heart's dark cage;
love isn't anything but a word on a wall.
It doesn't cook for you,
or go for walks,
or write a book,
or take your feelings into consideration.

We are all faithless and doomed,
more doomed for faithlessness
sub specie aeternitatis:
so let me say this,
and please feel free to pass it on:
heaven or nothingness,
we'll get there one day;
so leave some room, wherever it is,
for me.

Divorce

Driving home in rain,
Driven night-tides lash
The glass: witch lights
Wade and flash a blue horizon.

I am lost though the highway
Leads to home: each stepped
Pebbling of disaster hunches
Its exile in my mind.

Loud as moving earth,
Jethro Tull winds my blues
In pathways of desire,
And love and love and love.

The systematic whack
Of blades at raininess
Unravels the night:
It's night and where I am.

Did we ever stop to consider,
All litheness lost,
What happens to children?
Loss happens, loud as whisky.

The highway's a destination
Obscure as our lot, as laughter
Lost all the way home.
What will become of us?

WENDY WOODWARD

On the Diary of a German Woman in the Eastern Cape, circa 1840

Through the weft of her words,
we see a face in the candlelight
under a roof thatched too lightly
to stave off the rain, or the fear
of the dark and the aloes —
burning with their red lights
under the quiet moon.

She lives in the wilderness,
when all she wanted was a cedarwood kist
and a constant stove,
but what she found
was rain through the roof
onto her birthing bed,
umbrellas over her flickering body
to keep the baby from the rain.

And then delirium —
with spectres who smiled her into Hades,
which had the same greyness and drought
as the frontier her husband guarded
between the baboons and the leopards,
and the long-horned cattle pricking the air
far from the fat cows of green and daisied fields.

DAN WYLIE

Hornbill, Reactionary

The eye exists in the primitive state
André Breton

Stuff modernism, clacks Hornbill, the hell with angst
And its pessimistic mirrors on a journalist world!
To hell with the rootlessness of intellect,
The reflective razors of irony and the id,
The sawtooth taboos on sentiment and the soul.
I will not purge my voice of laughter or song:
I fly enfolded in the spirit of a place
Where fruit enjoys the tongue, the eye believes,
And the apocalyptic craft of a language of ribs
Has not yet cowed the celebrant.

There's a woman I watch
who walks in the forest and tenderly
lifts the alizarin fallen
mutsungunu leaves and holds them out
to glow in the sun
and carries them home to lay them
on the kitchen sill awhile;
she knows they are dying — of course
she knows — but she warms them
into the dark with her simple
admiration.

Hornbill's Wife

I have hidden my muse in the bole of the fig,
Walled her in with clay, just one eye showing,
The tip of her beak as I feed her.

Let her gestate.
How pretty she seems, how seductive, in her purdah!
How she stinks in there!

I accept this dutiful burden,
This abstinence, husbandhood, the daily migration
To the valley's foot for the choicest fruits.

I am content.
The nest becomes tight with growth
As my wings labour on the treadmill of seasons.

Winter Solstice

I
On this longest night of the year,
I am thought's hermaphrodite,
half present, half dreamt.

In this unreal world, all windows dissolve.
Sleep flounders between two stars:
orphaned halves of a press-stud.

Not knowing myself distresses the shadows of leaves.
I have admitted to my faults,
and still I am astonished to find myself sad!

Obsessed with truth, my heart
wrestles to conquer its cage.
To the south, an accumulating storm
accepts itself in spasms.

Content with duality, wood-owls confer:
Who? You.
Who? You.

II
Discovered by cold, I am
restless beneath these layers of rational wool.

Rhomboids of insomniac light are frozen to the walls.

Out in the real world, the wind is all bluster and muscle:
my every half-awakening dream is torn
by the shriek of a loosened latch.

On this longest night of the year,
the lumbar ache of loneliness is as integral to my being
as tinnitus is to hearing.

Eventually I rise, and pacify the latch.
In our mutual nudity, a streetlight laughs aloud.

Serene as a child in the traffic of her dreams,
the intuitive moon negotiates clouds.

III
At Newgrange, four thousand years gone, shamans,
astrologers, shaggy warriors, slaves, wrestled
massive boulders into place, built a tunnel,
a chamber, laid out chiefs' ashes, and nestled

beneath a mound their reverence, that acceptable dread.
Four thousand years on, this one winter dawn,
the sun still spikes the dark, horizon to tomb,
and gilds again the ethereal scabbards of the dead.

And here, the same sun, this identical dawn, tips
over the trees, lances through an airbrick, lights
roofbeam after beam, without shame, like a blade.

CATHY ZERBST

Beneath

Here, untidying the sun,
the fat shadows of leaves
are buttering the ground
Brown leaves, already fallen,
crouching and crunchy,
have collected at the edge of trees
in a dry wave
Only the patterns move
as the sun blinks
through gaps and spaces, seeking
the whole field

Always, there is a dying of leaves,
a dying of leaves
beneath the seemingly sure
pace of growing things
Always an implicit death of bones
beneath the healthy flesh
Always a nudity
beneath life's full apparel
And in the heart,
a starkness, a sickness
that grows from a need
for shade, for shelter
when the boughs are bare

From Dream to Reality

I have held you, swaying,
in the mind's brown marshy waters
like a reed

I have summoned you;
emerging like a lucid phantom,
from the core of my hope's whole shape

I have plaited you
thick, like a braid,
into my strands of night

I have spun you, webbed with want,
dangling you in the pith
of my dream's long branch

And after all this,
I am touched with the strange intangibility
of my need;

My hands are chalked with dust,
My limbs, chilled with doubt —

You have left me little choice
in this sky of solid earth,
in this sullen grave of truth

You Touch Me Only with Darkness

You touch me only with darkness;
with hands that slide away
like satin sheets,
                    shifting,
                    shifting into silence

I rise to greet my nights
like a pillar of ash
Each dream is a crushed petal,
leaving my fingers purple
with the bruised scent
of my own longing

I drown and drown
in waves of voiceless calling,
in tides, mute with desire

Your hands
are ripples in the fluid sky,
are quivers on the humming earth,
are something not for me;
                    not for my ridging back
                    not for my arching flesh

They touch me only with darkness
and slide away;
                    shifting,
                    shifting into silence

Together

We sit together in darkness,
gathered in loose folds
by low threads of light —
the last loops
that slip, before night descends
Time drawls
in a low contralto,
lulls the shadowed tides
of tired minds
and memory
What I see most clearly now —
your eyes
two edges
on the steep periphery
of rolling gloom
We occupy
a room that holds its sadness
like a gallant flower
We trace its perfume,
faint with breathing
Darkness pleats us in
with gentle deftness
as I take your hand

FIONA ZERBST

―ᴧᴧᴧᴧᴧᴧᴩᴩ◉ᴩᴩᴧᴧᴧᴧᴧᴧ―

Lost Lights

Night again
as curtains close on windows
and sink into their stillness in the cold.
No argument or knowledge
could release you
from staring at the sky,
the outer spiral,
of lights that waver out of definition.

But even when you let him go
you hold him here,
within the very force of contradiction.
Love is still the sadness —
if you call it love —
of never being able to
fulfil, erase, complete, infuse, destroy enough.

Night Swim

The cold sponge of seaweed
lies against my body,
drifts along the silence,
darkens as you touch me.

Vaguely I watch you
turning in the water,
swimming out before me,
blood-filled and light-held,

flensed from your history,
becoming this whalebone
trap of your longing.

You touch me, sounding.

Johannesburg

You've walked along
the beaten heat of workdays
where hawkers crowd around an old guitar;
the pavement fills
with hoarse, affronted voices
that sweat their heat and longing into tar.
The twist of wire
along the watered suburbs
becomes a dim periphery where some
seek out the rusted gate and hope to enter,
while others peddle ice-cream in the sun.

You've gone beyond
a hunger for belonging,
there's nothing here to which you could aspire.
You walk between this neon and that concrete,
a futureless perfection your desire.

Fire in the Evening

The road's lit by a narrow smudge
of heat. Even at this distance
wind's touched our faces with it,
met with our surprised resistance.

Yet we walk, into the dark,
nearer the wisped, uncertain fire
suffusing grass with knowledge that
tonight this field will have its hour.

We wait, wanting to see it spread,
see it rise against its pit —
char the air with orange as
the dark unhands the wholeness of it.

On Reading Ruth Miller

You died very slowly, so it seems.
Left us with strange emphases where death
becomes a line about to catch its breath
and life a certain hanging
by the nails.

An urge to darkness,
deafness to the surge
of star on star,
became the life you knew.
The words of you,
the ones that can be read,
pass deftly into this, the still unsaid.

NOTES ON CONTRIBUTORS

LIONEL ABRAHAMS was born in Johannesburg in 1928 and has worked as a poet, writer of fiction, critic, editor, publisher, and teacher of creative writing. He is the author of four volumes of poetry as well as a fictional work, *The Celibacy of Felix Greenspan*, which was recently reissued and acclaimed in the United States. He has received many awards.

TATAMKHULU AFRIKA was born in Sollum, Egypt, in 1920 of an Arab father and a Turkish mother. He was brought to South Africa in 1923, and was a prisoner of war for three years in Italy and Germany during the Second World War. After the war he worked for twenty years in Namibia as a miner. He settled in Cape Town in 1964, converted to Islam and joined the resistance to apartheid. He was arrested in 1987 for 'terrorism' and listed for five years as a banned person. The recipient of many prizes, he has published five volumes of poetry and one novel.

KEN BARRIS lives in Cape Town. His poetry has appeared in most of the literary journals in the country, and his first collection, *An Advertisement for Air* (Snailpress, 1993), won the Ingrid Jonker award. In 1990 he was the recipient of the first Sydney Clouts Memorial Award for poetry. He also writes fiction. *Small Change*, a collection of short stories (Ad Donker, 1988) won the AA Life/Ad Donker (Vita) award in the same year, and his short stories have appeared in various literary and mainstream magazines.

ROBERT BEROLD is the author of two collections of poetry, *The Door to the River* (1984) and *The Fires of the Dead* (1989). He was the editor of *People's Workbook* and since 1989 has edited the poetry journal *New Coin*. He has spent most of his working life in rural development, working with co-operatives and small enterprises. He lives on a communally owned farm near Grahamstown in the Eastern Cape.

JOOP BERSÉE was born in 1958 in Aerdenhout in Holland. After finishing school he worked in a museum in Haarlem from 1978 to 1988, during which time he started writing poetry in Dutch (some of it was published in Holland). He settled in South Africa in 1989 and has since studied theology and bookkeeping. He began writing in English in 1991 and his poems have been published in both South Africa and the UK.

DENNIS BRUTUS was born in 1924 in Salisbury (Harare), Rhodesia (Zimbabwe). He went to the United States in 1971 and was granted political asylum in 1983 after imprisonment on Robben Island for anti-apartheid activities. A celebrated poet who has won many awards, he teaches at the University of Pittsburgh. He has published several books of poetry, including *Sirens, Knuckles, Boots* (Mbari, 1963), *Letters to Martha and Other Poems from a South African Prison* (Heinemann, 1968), and *Stubborn Hope* (Three Continents, 1978).

LYNNE BRYER (1946-1994) was born and educated in the Eastern Cape, where she completed her MA in English at Rhodes University in 1969. After working in publishing in London and Cape Town, she launched her own company, Chameleon Press, in 1985. She managed her business alone while raising two children, and faced cancer with great courage. In 1991 she was awarded the AA Life Vita/Arthur Nortje Poetry Award.

CHERRY CLAYTON was born in Cape Town in 1943, and moved to Johannesburg in the late 1960s. She taught English at the University of the Witwatersrand and at the Rand Afrikaans University. Her major research has been on Olive Schreiner and South African women's writing. Her publications include *Olive Schreiner* (McGraw Hill, 1983) and *Women and Writing in South Africa: A Critical Anthology* (Heinemann, 1989). She has published poetry and short stories in literary journals in South Africa, England and Canada, and in South African anthologies. Her first poetry collection, *Leaving Home* (Snailpress and Red Kite Press, 1994), was awarded the CNA Prize for a best début volume in 1995. She teaches English and Women's Studies at the University of Guelph.

LISA COMBRINCK was born in Cape Town in 1967. She studied at the University of Cape Town and has worked as a journalist for the *Southern African Review of Books* and *South* newspaper. She is a national executive committee member of the Congress of South African Writers. A lecturer in English at Vista University, Mamelodi, her first collection of poetry, *The Woman is Too Heavy for the Poem*, is due at Deep South/ISEA, Grahamstown.

MIKE COPE was born in 1952, the son of writer Jack and painter Lesley. He spent his childhood at Clifton in the Cape and White River in the Eastern Transvaal. He matriculated in 1972 and has worked as a jeweller and a computer systems analyst. His volume of poetry, *Scenes and Visions*, was published by Snailpress in 1991. He lives and practises his trade in Mowbray, Cape Town.

PATRICK CULLINAN was born in Pretoria in 1932. After some education, mostly abroad, he farmed and ran a sawmill in the Eastern Transvaal. Apart from a lifelong commitment to poetry, he has also been a head-hunter (in Johannesburg), publisher (Bateleur Press), lecturer (University of the Western Cape), and magazine editor *(The Bloody Horse)*. His stories, poems and articles have appeared widely in South Africa and overseas. He has published four collections of poetry, a Lionel Abrahams anthology, and a major South African historical biography.

LEON DE KOCK was born in Mayfair, Johannesburg, in 1956. He was a graduate student at Rand Afrikaans University and Leeds University. He has been a reporter, reviewer and sub-editor and is currently a senior lecturer in English at the University of South Africa. He has published poetry, fiction, and criticism, and is the editor of a new critical journal, *scrutiny2*. He is the author of *Civilising Barbarians* (Witwatersrand University Press, 1995), and was awarded the 1995 Thomas Pringle prize for poetry.

INGRID DE KOK was born in 1951 and spent most of her childhood in Stilfontein, a mining town in the western Transvaal. She studied at the Universities of the Witwatersrand and Cape Town and at Queen's University in Canada. She is employed in the Department of Adult Education and Extra Mural Studies at the University of Cape Town. Her volume of poetry, *Familiar Ground* (Ravan Press, 1988) was reprinted in 1991. Her poetry has appeared in many South African anthologies and journals and in journals abroad. Individual poems have been translated into French, Spanish, Italian and Japanese. She is currently working on a poetry collection, tentatively titled *Transfer*.

GAIL DENDY was born in Durban. She has been SA gymnastics champion, a contemporary dancer and a choreographer. Her first poetry collection, *Assault and the Moth* (Greville Press Pamphlets, 1993), was followed by *People Crossing* (Snailpress,1995). A former lecturer at the University of South Africa, she holds an MA in Jewish Art. She now works as production editor on the *SA Law Journal* and is a freelance writer, editor and copywriter.

C.J. (JONTY) DRIVER was born in Cape Town in 1939. Educated at St Andrews, Grahamstown, and the University of Cape Town, he was President of the National Union of South African Students in 1963 and 1964. After a period in ninety-day detention, he left South Africa for England to teach at Sevenoaks College. While he was at Trinity College, Oxford, the South African authorities refused to renew his passport, and he became (for three years) stateless, and thereafter a British citizen. He was prohibited from returning to South Africa until the 1990s. He has worked as a teacher, housemaster, headmaster and principal at various schools in the United Kingdom and in Hong Kong. He has published four novels (two of which were banned in South Africa), a biography, and four books of poetry, the latest being *In the Water-Margins* (Snailpress and Crane River, 1994).

BASIL DU TOIT was born in Cape Town in 1951 and spent his childhood in Botswana. He went to Edinburgh in 1981 to study philosophy, and stayed on as a computer programmer. His first collection of poems, *Home Truths*, was published in 1988. He has a deep attachment to southern Africa as an ecological and historical zone.

JOHN EPPEL was born in 1947 in Lydenburg, South Africa. He teaches English at a secondary school in Bulawayo, where he lives. He has published three novels, *DGG Berry's The Great North Road*, which won the M-Net Prize for fiction, *Hatchings*, and *The Giraffe Man*. His poetry is collected in *Spoils of War* (Carrefour, 1989) and *Sonata for Matabeleland* (Snailpress and Baobab, 1995).

SHARI EPPEL was born in Harare in 1960 and has lived most of her life in southern Africa. She studied psychology at the University of Natal, Durban. Since then, she has taught maths, science and English to senior high school students in Bulawayo, Zimbabwe. She has a recently completed, unpublished novel and a second well under way.

FRANCIS FALLER was born in Cape Town in 1946 and moved to Pretoria, where he completed school and was employed in a law firm. He then turned to teaching, which has engaged him ever since in various parts of the country. He is currently Head of English, Johannesburg College of Education. His publications include two collections of poetry, *Weather Words* (Ad Donker, 1986), winner of the Vita Award, and *Verse-Over* (Carrefour, 1991), joint winner of the Sanlam Award.

GUS FERGUSON was born in Scotland in 1940, and has lived in South Africa since 1949. He is a cartoonist and poet who has published four collections of poetry, including *Snail Morning* (Ad Donker, 1979) and *Carpe Diem* (Carrefour, 1992). He is the proprietor of Snailpress and Firfield Pamphlet Press, has published *Slugnews* and recently launched a poetry magazine, *Carapace*.

JEREMY GORDIN was born in Pretoria in 1952 and lives in Johannesburg. From 1971 to 1975 he read English and philosophy at the Hebrew University of Jerusalem and studied with Israeli poet Dennis Silk. He then became a journalist for various South African newspapers. His publications include *With My Tongue in My Hand* (Heresy Press, 1981). He was managing director of Exclusive Books from 1983 to 1988 and was one of the winners of the 1987 Vita Poetry Prize.

STEPHEN GRAY was born in Cape Town in 1941 and educated at Cambridge and the Iowa Writers' Workshop. He lectured at the Rand Afrikaans University in Johannesburg for many years, becoming professor and head of department and took early retirement in 1991. His *Selected Poems* (1960-92) was published by David Philip in 1994. Other books of poetry include *Season of Violence* (Dangaroo, 1992) and *Taken* (Hond, 1995). His autobiography, *Accident of Birth*, was published by COSAW in 1993. In 1989 he edited *The Penguin Book of Southern African Verse*.

MICHAEL CAWOOD GREEN was born in Pinetown, Natal, in 1954. He was schooled there and in Tulare, California, as an exchange student. He worked as a stoker to finance his studies, and holds degrees from the University of Natal, Stanford University and the University of York. He now lectures in the Department of English at the University of Natal, Durban. His book *Resistant Form* is forthcoming at the Witwatersrand University Press. He has published scholarly essays and has released an album of original songs entitled *White Eyes*.

JAMES A. HARRISON was born in Cape Town in 1953. He is a biologist employed by the Avian Demography Unit at the

University of Cape Town, where he co-ordinates research projects. He is currently editing *The Atlas of Southern African Birds*. *New Contrast* and *Slugnews* have published his poetry.

DENIS HIRSON, born in 1951, left South Africa in 1973 when his father, who had been a political prisoner for nine years, was released and went into exile. He has lived in France since 1975, working as an actor and English teacher. His first prose work, *The House Next Door to Africa*, was published in 1986 by David Philip and has subsequently been translated into French and Italian. He has translated a selection of Breyten Breytenbach's poetry, *In Africa Even the Flies are Happy* (1977), and co-edited *The Heinemann Book of South African Short Stories* (1994). He is currently working on an anthology of South African poetry for Longman Publishers.

EVELYN JOHN HOLTZHAUSEN is Night Editor and Books Editor of the *Cape Times* newspaper. Born in Germiston in 1950, he has worked as a journalist in South Africa, Swaziland, Britain and Norway for the past 25 years. His poems have been published widely in literary magazines in South Africa and elsewhere.

CHRISTOPHER HOPE was born in 1944 in Johannesburg. He studied at the Universities of the Witwatersrand and Natal, and is a full-time writer resident in France. He is the recipient of many South African and international awards, and has published novels, poetry, plays, non-fiction, and books for children. His novels include *A Separate Development* (Ravan, 1980), *Kruger's Alp* (Heinemann, 1984), and *My Chocolate Redeemer* (Heinemann, 1989).

PETER HORN was born in Teplitz-Schoenau in 1934 and educated in Germany and South Africa. He is professor of German at the University of Cape Town. He has published six volumes of poetry, among them *Walking Through Our Sleep* (1974), *Silence in Jail* (1979), and *An Axe in the Ice* (1993). He has written two volumes of essays on South African poetry and has received several prizes.

ALLAN KOLSKI HORWITZ was born in 1952 in Vryburg. He grew up in Cape Town and studied philosophy and literature at the University of Cape Town. He has worked in the trade union and civic movements. He published *Call from the Free State* in 1979, and substantial portions of his work have been included in two anthologies. He is a member of the Botsotso Poetry and Publishing Group.

ALAN JAMES published the poetry journal *Upstream* in the mid-1980s from Cape Town before emigrating to Australia in 1992. He has a legal training and is the author of *At a Railhalt* (1981), *Producing the Landscape* (Upstream, 1987), and *Morning near Genadendal* (Snailpress, 1992), among others.

DAISY JONES was born in England in 1970. She came to South Africa with her parents in 1976 and has studied at the Universities of Cape Town and Witwatersrand. She began work as a junior reporter for *The Star* in August 1995. Her work has appeared in literary journals in South Africa.

RUSTUM KOZAIN was born in Paarl in 1966. He studied at the University of Cape Town. He has published several poems and articles in South Africa, the UK and France, and has read poetry in South Africa, France and Northwest Ohio.

DOUGLAS LIVINGSTONE is a marine biologist who works in Durban. He has published many volumes of poetry, including *The Skull in the Mud* (1960), *A Rosary of Bone* (1975, 1983) and *A Littoral Zone* (1991). He is widely regarded as one of the foremost living poets in South Africa.

MOIRA LOVELL studied at the Universities of Cape Town and Natal. She is head of the English Department at the Wykeham Collegiate School in Pietermaritzburg. Her poetry has been published in many journals and anthologies. Her collection, *Out of the Mist*, was published by Snailpress in 1994. In addition, she has published short stories and has written a number of plays. *The Entertainer* won the Enact Playwright Award in 1990.

ROD MACKENZIE was born in Durban in 1963. He studied at the University of Cape Town and Rhodes University and has taught English at Langa High School in Cape Town. A volume of poems, *Gathering Light*, was published in 1992 (Snailpress). He currently works in human resource development in Johannesburg.

DON MACLENNAN was born in London in 1929 and came to South Africa in 1938. He has spent most of his working life as a teacher, both in South Africa and in the United States, retiring in 1994 from Rhodes University after twenty-nine years there. He has published a number of plays, short stories, six collections of poems, including *Letters* (Carrefour, 1992) and *The Poetry Lesson* (Snailpress, 1995), and a handful of scholarly works.

MZI MAHOLA was born Mzikayise Winston Mahola in Alice in 1949, moving to Port Elizabeth in 1954. He started writing poetry in 1974, but his first manuscript was confiscated by the Bureau of State Security in 1976. He started writing again in 1988 and his work has been published in many journals and newsletters. He has contributed to five anthologies, and his first collection, *Strange Things*, was published by Snailpress in 1994. He works for the Port Elizabeth Museum.

CHRIS MANN is a leading South African poet who recently joined the Grahamstown Foundation after more than a decade in rural and peri-urban development at The Valley Trust on the outskirts of Durban. His recent work includes *South Africans: A Series of Portrait Poems* (Natal University Press, 1995). He is married to the painter Julia Skeen, who is currently working with him on an extended series of painting-poems.

JULIA MARTIN was born in 1959 in Durban and grew up in Pietermaritzburg. After studying at Natal University, she moved to Cape Town in 1981 to teach English at the University of Cape Town. Since 1985 she has taught in the English Department at the University of the Western Cape. She writes story essays and poems, and makes ceramic sculptures.

PAUL MASON was born in Hillbrow in 1963 and grew up in Johannesburg. He studied at the Universities of the Witwatersrand, Cape Town and Natal. He has published poetry and reviews in literary journals and lives in Cape Town, where he lectures in English.

ZAKES MDA is the pen-name of Professor Zanemvula Kizito Gatyeni Mda, playwright, painter and film-maker. As an academic he has worked at the National University of

Lesotho, Yale University, University of Vermont, and the University of the Witwatersrand. He lives in Johannesburg where he works full-time as a writer, painter and director of both theatre and film.

JOAN METELERKAMP was born in 1956 and grew up in the Natal midlands. She studied acting at the University of Cape Town, and worked for a short time in educational theatre before returning to English studies. She has taught English at the Universities of Natal and the Western Cape. Her first collection of poetry, *Towing the Line* (Carrefour, 1991), was joint winner of the 1991 Sanlam literary award.

KOBUS MOOLMAN was born in Pietermaritzburg in 1964. He studied at the University of Natal and worked for a time as a newspaper sub-editor and a teacher in black education. He is Education Officer at the Tatham Art Gallery in Maritzburg. His poetry has been published in literary magazines in South Africa and elsewhere. In 1988 he won the BBC African Theatre Award. In 1991 he was awarded the Macmillan Southern African Playwriting Award, and was runner-up in the Amstel Playwright of the Year Award in 1992.

SEITLHAMO MOTSAPI grew up in Bela-Bela, near Warm-baths in the Transvaal. He has degrees from the Universities of the Witwatersrand and the North, where he now lectures in English. He has published poetry in literary journals and his first volume, *earthstepper/the ocean is very deep*, was published by ISEA in 1994.

SALLY-ANN MURRAY was born in 1961 in Durban. A lecturer in the Department of English at the University of Natal, she has published one collection of poetry, *Shifting*

(Carrefour, 1991), which was a joint winner of the 1991 Sanlam literary award.

ANDRIES WALTER OLIPHANT was born in Heidelberg, Transvaal. Educated at the Universities of the Western Cape and Oregon, he is a poet, writer of fiction, publisher and critic, and has been an editor of the journal *Staffrider*, as well as a general editor of the publishing division of the Congress of South African Writers. He has played a leading role in the National Arts Coalition, and has won several literary prizes. His publications include *At the End of the Day* (Justified Press, 1988) and *The Change of Season and Other Stories* (1995).

KAREN PRESS lives in Cape Town and is a writer of poetry and children's stories. She has worked in alternative education projects, helped to found a publishing collective, and is employed as an editor of fiction for young adults. She has published three collections of poetry, *This Winter Coming* (Cinnamon Crocodile), *Bird Heart Stoning the Sea* (Buchu Books), and *The Coffee Shop Poems* (Snailpress).

ARJA SALAFRANCA was born in Malaga, Spain, in 1971. She has had short stories published in *The Finishing Touch*, a COSAW anthology of stories gleaned from the 1991 Nadine Gordimer Award, as well as in *Lyf-Spel/Body Play*, an anthology of erotic stories. Her poetry has been published in journals and anthologies. In 1994 she won the Sanlam literary award for an unpublished collection of poetry, *A Life Stripped of Illusions.* She lives in Johannesburg and works as a journalist.

BARBARA SCHREINER, a descendant of Olive Schreiner, is a feminist, eco-socialist and writer who lives in Johannesburg.

Her publications include *My Spirit is Not Banned: The Story of Francis Baard* (Zimbabwe Publishing House, 1987) and *The Gossiping Grass* (Macmillan Boleswa, 1993). She has written plays and contributed to film scripts, and is an environmental activist.

ADAM SCHWARTZMAN was born in Johannesburg in 1973. After matriculating in South Africa, he attended Charterhouse in England and travelled, spending eight months in Paris. He is currently reading English at Pembroke College, Oxford. His poems have appeared in journals and anthologies, and are collected in *The Good Life. The Dirty Life. and other stories* (Carcanet and Snailpress, 1995).

BONGANI SITOLE is an oral poet who lives near Umtata. He rose to prominence in the old Transkei after the release of Nelson Mandela. He worked as a research assistant at the University of Transkei but is now retired.

DOUGLAS REID SKINNER was born in the Northern Cape town of Upington in 1949. He has worked in computer information systems in England and America. He edited *Upstream, New Contrast* and *The South African Literary Review,* and directed The Carrefour Press from 1988 to 1992. He has published four collections of poems, among them *The Unspoken* (Carrefour, 1988) and *The Middle Years* (Carrefour, 1993). He currently lives in London.

KELWYN SOLE was born in 1951 and is a lecturer in English at the University of Cape Town. He has published *The Blood of Our Silence* (Ravan, 1988), and *Projections in the Past Tense* (Ravan, 1992). He has been awarded the Olive Schreiner prize and the Sydney Clouts award for poetry and has produced many critical articles as well as a doctorate on black South African writing.

WILMA STOCKENSTRÖM was born in 1933 at Napier, Western Cape. She studied at the University of Stellenbosch, and has worked as an actress and translator. Her first publication, a volume of poetry entitled *Vir die Bysiende Leser*, appeared in 1970. This was followed by five further volumes of poetry, five novels, and one play. Formerly resident in Pretoria, she now lives in Cape Town.

MARK SWIFT left South Africa in 1986 and is employed as a senior sub-editor on the *Cambridge Evening News* in England. His poems, prose and criticism have been published in newspapers and in many literary magazines and anthologies in South Africa and in England. His first collection, *Treading Water*, won the Ingrid Jonker Prize for the best début volume in southern Africa. His second book, *Gentlewoman* (with photographs by Sigurd Olivier), had a long history of banning and unbanning in South Africa and was also published in New York. His third collection, *Seconds Out*, was published in 1983. In 1987 he was awarded the Thomas Pringle prize for poetry. Swift has completed a new volume of poems, *Making Tracks* (Snailpress and Crane River, 1996), and an experimental novel.

IAN TROMP was born in 1969 in Johannesburg. An art historian by training, he is presently involved in a visual-literacy training programme. He has published one volume of poetry, *Setting Out* (Snailpress, 1994), and has published poems in various international journals. He was the recipient of the Ernst van Heerden poetry prize in 1990.

MATTHEW VAN DER WANT was born in Johannesburg in 1972. He studied at the University of the Witwatersrand and is a singer/songwriter. His songs have been recorded by Shifty Records and his début CD is due for release.

CHRIS VAN WYK was born in 1957 in Soweto, and lives in Riverlea, Johannesburg. He was co-founder of the literary journal *Wietie*, and edited *Staffrider* for several years. He has published a wide range of writing, including fiction, poetry and criticism.

PETER WILHELM was born in Cape Town in 1943. His father was a naval officer and his mother a medical doctor. He has published two collections of poetry, three collections of short stories, and four novels. His most recent novel, *The Mask of Freedom*, won the 1995 Sanlam Prize. He is at present Cape editor of the *Financial Mail*.

WENDY WOODWARD grew up in the Eastern Cape and teaches at the University of the Western Cape. At present she is conducting research into women on the borders of early nineteenth century colonial South Africa. Her book of poems, *Seance for the Body*, was published in 1994 by Snailpress.

DAN WYLIE was born and raised in Zimbabwe. He was conscripted into the (then) Rhodesian army. He studied at Rhodes University, Grahamstown, and, after six years as wanderer, secondary school teacher, hermit and oddjobber, returned there. He has published poetry and scholarly articles.

CATHY ZERBST was born in the Cape in 1959. She has worked as a singer, composer and musical director, and her poems have been published in literary journals. She lives in

Johannesburg where she works as an editor for an educational publishing company.

Fiona Zerbst was born in Cape Town in 1969 and studied at the University of Cape Town. She is a freelance journalist. Her first book of poetry, *Parting Shots*, was published by Carrefour in 1991. *The Small Zone* was published by Snailpress in 1995. In 1990 she was jointly awarded the AA Life Vita/ Arthur Nortje award for poems published in *Upstream* magazine. She lives in the Ukraine.

COPYRIGHT ACKNOWLEDGEMENTS

The editors and publisher gratefully acknowledge the following persons and instances for permission to use poems in this anthology:

Ad Donker and the author for the poem by Bongani Sitole, Russell Kaschula for the translation; *New Coin* and the author for the poem by Denis Hirson; *New Coin*, Snailpress and the author for poems by Lionel Abrahams; *New Coin*, *New Contrast* and the author for poems by Tatamkhulu Afrika; *New Contrast*, Snailpress and the author for poems by Ken Barris; Robert Berold for his poems; *New Coin* and the author for poems by Joop Bersée; *Staffrider*, *Soho Square* (Bloomsbury) and the author for poems by Dennis Brutus; Georgia Bryer, Carrefour Press and *New Contrast* for poems by Lynne Bryer; Snailpress, Red Kite Press and the author for poems by Cherry Clayton; *Staffrider* and the author for poems by Lisa Combrinck; Snailpress, *New Coin* and the author for poems by Mike Cope; Snailpress and the author for poems by Patrick Cullinan; *New Contrast* and the author for poems by Leon de Kock; *Southern African Review of Books*, *New Coin*, *New Contrast* and the author for poems by Ingrid de Kok; Snailpress and the author for poems by Gail Dendy; *New Contrast* and the author for poems by C.J. Driver; *New Coin*, *New Contrast* and the author for poems by Basil du Toit; *New Coin*, *New Contrast* and the author for poems by John Eppel; *New Contrast* and the author for poems by Shari Eppel; the author for poems by Francis Faller; *New Contrast* and *Sesame* for poems by Gus Ferguson; the author for poems by Jeremy Gordin; *New Contrast*, *Staffrider*, *Kunapipi*, Dangaroo Press and the author for poems by Stephen Gray; the author for poems by Michael Cawood Green; *New Contrast* and the author for poems by James A. Harrison; *Soho Square* and the author for the poem by Evelyn Holtzhausen; *New Contrast* and the author for the poem by Christopher Hope; The Congress of South African Writers and the author for poems by Peter Horn; *New Coin* and the author for the poem by Allan Kolski Horwitz; Snailpress and the author for poems by Alan James; *New Contrast* and the author for the poem by Daisy Jones; *New Coin* and the author for the poem by Rustum Kozain; Carrefour Press and the author for the poem by Douglas Livingstone; Snailpress and the author for the poem by Moira Lovell; *New Contrast* and Snailpress for the poems by Rod Mackenzie; Snailpress and the author for poems by Don Maclennan; Snailpress and the author for poems by Mzi Mahola; *New Coin, New Contrast,* University of Natal Press and the author for poems by Chris Mann; *New Coin* and the author for poems by Julia Martin; *Sesame* and the author for the poem by Paul Mason; *Staffrider* and the author for the poem by Zakes Mda; *Sesame*, Carrefour Press, *New Coin* and the author for poems by Joan Metelerkamp; *New Contrast* and the author for poems by Kobus Moolman; *Staffrider, New Coin,* the Institute for the Study of English in Africa and the author for poems by Seitlhamo Motsapi; Carrefour Press and the author for the poem by Sally-Ann Murray; *Kunapipi, New Contrast* and the author for poems by Andries Walter Oliphant; *New Coin, New Contrast* and the author for poems by Karen Press; *New Coin* and the author for the poem by Arja Salafranca; *New Coin* and the author for the poem by Barbara Schreiner; Carcanet Press and the author for poems by Adam Schwartzman; Carrefour Press and the author for poems by Douglas Reid Skinner; *Southern African Review of Books*, Ravan Press and the author for poems by Kelwyn Sole; *Soho Square*